In So Many Words

First published in 2002 by Mercier Press
Douglas Village Cork
Tel: (021) 489 9858; Fax: (021) 489 9887
E.mail: books@mercierpress.ie
16 Hume Street Dublin 2
Tel: (01) 661 5299; Fax: (01) 661 8583
E.mail: books@marino.ie
Web: www.mercier.ie

Trade enquiries to CMD Distribution
55A Spruce Avenue
Stillorgan Industrial Park
Blackrock County Dublin
Tel: (01) 294 2560; Fax: (01) 294 2564
E.mail: cmd@columba.ie

© Con Houlihan 2002

ISBN 1 85635 393 1
10 9 8 7 6 5 4 3 2

A CIP record for this title is available
from the British Library

Cover design by Marino Books
Set in Goudy
Printed in Ireland by ColourBooks,
Baldoyle Industrial Estate, Dublin 13

IN SO MANY WORDS
THE BEST OF CON HOULIHAN

MERCIER PRESS

CONTENTS

REFLECTIONS ON A LIFETIME IN PRINT

I have been in journalism for more years than I care to forget – now read on . . .

Before I reached double figures in age, I had pieces published in the famous weekly magazine called the *Champion*.

It came to our town on the second train every Friday – in time to be in Davy Griffin's shop down by the railway station when we were released from school.

It cost three very old pennies – and if you think that was only peanuts, you do not know the history of Ireland's economy.

To assemble those three old pennies every week necessitated multifarious activities, not all legal; I always succeeded.

The *Champion* is long since part of history or at least folklore; for me it has bequeathed fond and loving memories . . .

It was printed in Farringdon Street, a narrow thoroughfare where central London hadn't quite ended and where East London hadn't quite begun.

When first I went to London, I lost no time in seeking out Farringdon Street.

The Holy Father had yet to visit Ireland and kneel down and kiss the tarmac – but on that day long ago I felt like making a similar gesture.

My next involvement in the sacred craft came when I

was incarcerated in a boarding school set in the woodlands of East Cork.

The regime was not only Spartan but dictatorial – action was required. And so came the birth of an underground movement; it was peaceful, more or less . . .

Of course, we had a paper; it was called the *College Courier*; I was its proud editor.

We wrote by hand – very longhand, that is. Only one copy was published – clandestinely, of course.

And it had illustrations: a brilliant lad from Belfast did the cartoons – you will be relieved to hear that he went on to become a luminary in the British civil service.

A great time was had by all – until one night in the study hall I got a tap on the shoulder from a grim-faced priest. He conducted me to the superior's study; there I was told about the error of my ways.

And for good measure I was formally told that I was getting the red card – in layman's language, I was expelled.

I looked forward with less than pleasant thoughts to the prospect of being driven in an unmarked car to the railway station at dawn.

Don't tell me about free speech: there ain't no such thing.

It cost me my scholarship – and, in all probability, my place as captain of the Football team in the following year.

I hasten to add, however, that like my sister, Edith Piaf, I have no regrets.

XPress, 2 June 1995

Phoning Home

When I was attempting to grow up in rural Ireland, telephones were not few and far between – outside the towns there weren't any. I was entitled to vote before ever I made a phone call.

My generation knew phones from the screen only. They were mostly two-piece instruments: you put one piece to your better ear and spoke into the other piece.

When I was teaching in Knockaderry National School, there was such a phone in Sonny Ulick O'Sullivan's pub in the nearby village of Farranfore. It was in excellent working order.

I used to avail of it most days of the week to send bets to my friendly bookmaker in Castle Island. There were days when I was sorry that the phone was in such good order – but that's another story.

One of the most piquant stories in the history of the GAA concerns an All-Ireland semi-final between Kerry and Cavan at a time when communications were far from good.

The effects of the so-called Civil War still lingered. Bridges had been blown up. Telephone poles and wires had been torn down. The young State was in chaos.

The game was in Tralee. Few people travelled from Cavan. Money was scarce. There was no public transport and little private transport. A man in the town of Cavan kept racing pigeons; he and a few friends took them to Tralee.

Back at home there was intense excitement. It grew even more intense as the afternoon wore on. By about five o'clock you could see young lads perched on rooftops, straining their eyes southwards.

The evening was turning into dusk when cries of excitement told that the pigeons were coming – and so they were. The gallant birds had evaded all their enemies, natural and unnatural.

Soon they were hovering over their loft. No time was lost in getting the little bits of paper that brought the news. A sad silence ensued – Cavan had lost by a point.

This was an occasion on which there was no impulse to kill the messengers that brought the bad news.

The story recalls a chapter from the heyday of bare-knuckle fighting in these islands. A member of the Jewish community in the East End of London was champion of Britain in the middle of the nineteenth century; his name was Daniel Mendoza.

Boxing was then illegal and fights took place at secret venues, mostly in half-hidden meadows, not too far from some big city. When Mendoza fought away from home, his minders took with them two pigeons – a black and a white.

Daniel was an icon to the people of the East End. On the occasion of every fight the news was eagerly awaited in Whitechapel and the Mile End Road and Stepney and Limehouse and Bethnal Green and beyond.

The local hero went unbeaten for years. The white pigeon circling above its loft was a familiar sight. Then one sad day the black pigeon came into view – Daniel was champion no more.

If you are familiar with the writing of Arnold Bennett, you will know that the pigeons were used by newspapers, especially evening papers, before the coming of the phone.

A reporter would take two with him: one took back the half-time score, the other took the final tally.

I remember an occasion when the people in my neighbourhood were like the natives of East London in the days of Daniel Mendoza. Our local hero was a greyhound that was running in the Irish Cup in Clounanna.

By the third day he was in the semi-final. That evening about fifty people were gathered at the gate of the avenue that led to the owner's house.

When we saw the lights of the car approaching about an hour after the meeting had ended, we didn't have to be told the news. If our hero had won, his connections wouldn't have been in any hurry home.

I grew up in an age of very poor communications; it was rather ironic that eventually I worked at a trade where speed in communications was essential.

I will always remember that night in Genoa when Packie Bonner saved and David O'Leary scored in that famous penalty shoot-out. The phone in my bedroom was on the blink and I had to search desperately for a phone that worked.

I found one in a dark cubby under a stairs; I couldn't read my notes but I had plenty of facts in my head to send back to Dublin. I was so exhausted afterwards that I took little part in the celebrations.

Indeed, there was hardly any celebration – we were all too exhausted, including the players.

I will long remember too that midday in Barcelona when

Wayne McCullough took silver and Michael Carruth took gold. The fights took place in the run-down township of Badalona; communications weren't great.

Rather than wait indefinitely for a phone, I decided to get back to my base, but it was about three miles away and on that steamy morning I didn't feel like walking or running. I went in search of a taxi.

Alas, I should have known better. The Catalans, like the rest of the Spanish, look on lunchtime as sacred. There wasn't a taxi to be found. Eventually one came along and dropped off a demure lady.

I could have embraced her; instead I stood in front of the taxi so that it couldn't move. The driver shouted *'Cena!'*; I shouted *'Moneta!'* I won.

The mobile phone didn't come a day too soon.

LAS VEGAS IN A FIELD NEAR CLONDALKIN

Now it can be told: about twenty years ago I was invited to a travellers' wedding, one of the few infidels ever to enjoy the privilege. There was no mystery about the invitation: I had been their ombudsman and amanuensis for a good many years.

The ombudsman part consisted mainly in pleading for leniency from local farmers who didn't look too kindly on having their gates lifted from the hinges so that travellers' horses could enjoy a night of illicit grass.

As amanuensis I had to deal mainly with the Department of Social Welfare and a certain Hector Grey.

Anyhow, it was a special wedding; the singing was especially great; if you have ever heard Margaret Barry, you will appreciate the passion which the travelling people bring to their songs.

Since I came to Dublin, I have more or less lost touch with the travellers; if I meet any of them, it is usually in mid-December – some of my old neighbours come up to sell holly and Christmas trees.

And so I knew nothing about a remarkable event which took place last week – until it was all over.

Jim Byrne, God rest him, for many years mine host of the Hideout in Kilcullen and the most inventive publican that ever pulled a pint, would have relished the afore-mentioned event.

13

Once upon a time he planned to stage a 'repeat' of the famous Donnelly–Cooper fight – in, of course, Donnelly's Hollow.

It was to be the highlight of a local pageant – but, for a variety of reasons, it fell through.

Anyhow, it wouldn't have been 'for real' but a fight that took place last week in a field near Clondalkin certainly was.

The protagonists were two young men of the traveller tribe; the fight, far from being impromptu, was well organised.

I do not know if there was a ring; I know that it was a bare-knuckle fight.

And that brought a whiff of the nineteenth century, of the great days when Mace and Gully and Sayers and their fellows enjoyed the prestige reserved for professional footballers now.

William Hazlitt should have been in that field near Clondalkin last week; Pierce Egan would have been enthralled.

There was a crowd of about five hundred to watch the two young pugilists – and of course some busybody alerted the gardai.

They came but could do nothing. How could they when they had to deal with a frenzy of women and children . . .

The fight ran its course. Eventually the gardai carted the two combatants off to the hospital; they were treated for cuts and bruises and went back to the bosoms of their families.

What a pity that someone wasn't perched up in a tree with a movie camera – it would have made great television.

Another source of great television also went to waste last week.

This was not in a field near Clondalkin but on a mountainside in Wales.

The protagonists were the local foresters and about five hundred wild goats.

Goats, as we all know, have an extremely catholic taste in food; they may not eat everything in sight but they go as near as makes little difference.

And seemingly the goats on the slopes of Snowdon do no good for the trees.

And so one day last week the foresters assembled in considerable numbers and set out to round up the nannies and the billies.

They were armed with what seemed a foolproof plan: the goats would be funnelled into a gully where a net would do the rest.

And then the goats would be transported up to a part of the Highlands where there are no trees to damage – we were not told what the good people of Scotland did to deserve all this.

Anyhow, the bould foresters set to work armed with two-way radios: the goats would have to fight bare-handed.

The head of the party issued a remarkable rallying cry a few moments before the kick-off: 'If a billy goat comes at you, just shout at him – and he will stop.'

The good man may know a great deal about trees but his knowledge of goats seems to be rather sketchy – as some of his round-up party found out to their cost.

The score at the end of a long and arduous day was: Injured Foresters 17, Captured Goats 0.

As night began to descend, the goats were high up on the top of a disused slate quarry whither no human could pursue them – and they were laughing their heads and their horns off.

The head forester is alleged to have said that they should be shot – he seems to be a bad loser.

My guess is that there will be a replay – watch this space.

It all reminds me of a famous story which I have told here before.

It is set in Paris about twenty years ago and is absolutely authentic. The protagonists were the local pigeons – thousands and thousands of them – and the city fathers.

The latter were under ever-increasing pressure from local spoilsports who objected to the pigeons' penchant for aerial bombardment.

And so one Monday morning they scattered grain all around the fair city, grain that was dressed with sleeping powder.

And that evening the dozy pigeons – thousands and thousands of them – were transported over to the Vosges in unmarked vans. The spoilsports were happy – until about three o'clock on the Thursday afternoon.

The sky began to darken over Montmartre and the Madeleine and the Arc de Triomphe, not to mention the Rue Haussmann and the Opera and the Place de Carousel – the pigeons were back.

Evening Press, 8 December 1989

Gone Fishin'

Daydreaming is good for you, but if Big Brother could, he would employ some electronic device for detecting it – and he would take the necessary action.

For the time being we are free to indulge our fantasies – and I am back in London in the seventeenth century.

England's capital was then only a modest town built mainly along by the Thames.

What is now Soho was a marsh where hares were coursed. When you went to what is now Hyde Park, you were out in the country.

Izaak Walton was a citizen of that riverside town. He was born in Stafford in 1593; by 1624 he was settled in London as a linen draper.

When you read *The Compleat Angler*, the book that made Walton immortal, you become convinced that he lived in an era of peace and tranquillity.

It wasn't quite that way: he lived in an age of violent upheaval; the struggle between the King and the middle classes culminated in January 1644.

Charles paid with his head on a scaffold, on a morning when a blizzard raged – he went into folklore as 'the Snow King'.

Walton's great book appeared four years after that momentous event but it doesn't contain the slightest hint of the turbulent times in which it was written.

The Compleat Angler is often called the fisherman's bible; it is much more than that.

It is a symphony that evokes rural England as consummately as did John Constable's paintings two hundred years later.

Interspersed amidst the discourses on angling you will find little poems and snatches of old songs and country sayings and observations on the rural way of life.

Walton's book is a shining example of Coleridge's belief that writers retain the eye of childhood in maturity.

I was a member of Izaak Walton's brotherhood long before I heard of him or his great book.

I was about nine when I caught my first trout; from that moment you could say that I was hooked.

I suppose that my love of angling came from my obsession with water. Like many small boys, I loved playing with it because it is more malleable even than sand.

I got great satisfaction from turning streamlets out of their course and making little lakes and canals and dams.

I was then still too young to be allowed near a river on my own lest my love of water make me too bold and I be swept down to the Atlantic.

On that famous day when I caught my first trout, I was on my own – if you exclude a few terriers of dubious ancestry.

Nine may have seemed a tender age to be fishing on a river in a flood, but parents in that generation hadn't become aware of American child psychology and sensed that a watched pot doesn't boil.

My heartwater was in Gleannsharoon River. It originates about four miles north-east of Castle Island under a hill called Crinna which is a miniature version of South Africa's Table Mountain.

For the first mile of its course it runs through what was once woodland; for the rest of its journey it flows between fertile fields. It meets up with the Maine about a quarter of a mile west of the town.

It is almost twenty-five years since I fished that river, but without delving very deep into my memory I could draw a map of it from its source to its merger with the Maine.

I could mark in all the runs and the pools and the shallows and the depths and the places where trout love to abide and the places that they shun.

I know that there are a few members of my generation who could do the same but perhaps I could go one better – I would draw the line above which fluke do not travel.

That is the local name for freshwater flounder. They will not take up residence unless the bed is sandy.

On the occasion of a flood, I loved to be up before the dawn and be at the river by first light.

On those days I partook of the empty Irish breakfast – a cup of tea. Time was precious.

And I never took with me any kind of food or drink. I could go the whole day without thinking of sustenance.

When a hen is hatching, she is much the same: all she needs is a little dish of water – and a fistful of sand to scour her maw.

The legacy of those unlost days remains with me, sometimes to the amazement of my travelling companions.

On those days of pilgrimage from Dublin to Killarney for the Munster Final, my companions always agreed with

Napoleon – an army travels on its stomach.

When we went by road, they ate on the way down, had a snack (about three hamburgers a man) in Killarney, and ate again on the way home.

While all this was going on, I would be content with a few drinks – and I could hear my companions thinking, 'What manner of man is this?'

Samuel Johnson used to say that his happiest hours were those spent in bed when he should have been up; many of my happiest hours were with the waters and the wild.

There were days when the water was alive and there were days when the fish were 'down' and you could go for hours without getting an answer.

The most satisfying days of all were those when the take was slow and you had to work hard to get a few fish.

At the end of your endeavours you felt like a man who had batted all day on a bad wicket to garner about thirty precious runs.

And of course there was the camaraderie. You meet a better class of rogue by the river: I have yet to know an angler who was a totally bad man.

And if an angler tells you that the river washes away your cares, believe him: Izaak Walton found peace by the water during the throes of that bitter and bloody Civil War.

Even the most dedicated follower of Dublin's Gaelic Football team would find solace from rod and line.

Izaak Walton bequeathed an immortal one-liner to his disciples. He summed up in a few words the advisability of keeping well back from the water and using the lightest tackle feasible: 'far off and fine'.

My dear departed friend Danny Horan, World War veteran, admirer of French women, aficionado of Rugby, sweet singer, and a great deal more, was the best trout angler that I ever knew.

He too left behind him an immortal one-liner which Izaak Walton would have cherished: 'You must know what the fish are thinking.'

CRYING WOLFE

Two men surnamed Wolfe became famous in American writing in the twentieth century: Tom Wolfe was basically a journalist; Thomas Wolfe was a novelist.

Tom's semi-novel, *The Bonfire of the Vanities*, made him famous. He is a member of our generation. He is a native of the Deep South. So was Thomas. He grew up with the century and died at thirty-eight. He achieved great fame but is now half-forgotten.

He was a turgid writer. He wrote an enormous amount and can be difficult to read but he rewards you now and then with an unforgettable observation, such as: 'The most evocative of all American sounds is the whistle of a distant train.'

If you were asked to nominate its Irish counterpart, what would you say? It all depends of course on your background. If you grew up in a seaport, it might be the siren of an incoming ship.

If you grew up in a suburb, it might be the sounds made by the milkman on his rounds in the early morning. If you grew up in rural Ireland a generation ago, it might be the lowing of cattle being driven to the fair in what Thomas Hardy called the non-human hours.

That world has almost totally disappeared now. It was there for a very long time and if some brave composer ever attempts to base a symphony on it, it should include that loneliest and most haunting of sounds.

The fair now is almost totally a thing of the past. A few survive, notably in Killorglin and Buttevant and Ballycastle, but the mart now is becoming more and more dominant.

On a fair morning long ago you would see lights coming on in houses at such a crazy hour that you wondered if people were getting up or going to bed.

There was always a tradition of early rising in rural Ireland. People used to say: 'If you miss an hour in the morning, you will never catch up with it in the course of the day.'

Even on an ordinary morning you can hear something like this: 'In the name of God, get up. 'Tis five o'clock. There isn't a cow milked or a child washed or a pig fed.'

Thus spoke the woman of the house. Of course she exaggerated but there was method in her clarion call. It was real on a fair morning, except that for five o'clock you would substitute four or even three.

Usually, there was an additional call: 'By the time you get to the town, the fair will be over.' It was hardly an occasion for the traditional Irish breakfast.

The black pudding was forgotten, not to mention the white pudding. There was no honey and brown bread, nor was there a sloe-eyed colleen sitting at the spinning wheel and singing 'The Coolin'.

There was nothing romantic about rounding up the cattle in the early hours. It wasn't at all like what you see in movies about the Old West. There was no cracking of whips and camp cooks shouting: 'Come and get it!'

Instead there was a great deal of cursing and swearing until at last you got the unwilling beasts on the road to the fair. Even then your troubles weren't over: some cows can spot a hole in a fence as quickly as Mickey Sheehy could spot the chance of a goal.

The mind games have started. The tanglers are working for the big jobbers and are trying to create the state of the market.

Eventually you get to the fair, but not before sharp exchanges on the way. They make fake bids for your cattle. They have no more notion of buying than you have of selling.

When you get to the town, your next aim is to take up a good position – that's the whole point in coming so early.

For generations, the fairs in Castle Island were among the most famous in the country. It was an ideal location in the middle of a fertile valley, inhabited mainly by hard-working small farmers.

The two biggest fairs were those of November Day and New Year's Day. There were fairs every month but those two were so big that they hardly fitted in the town.

The horses and cabs and ponies were always stationed at what was known as the top of the town. This was the eastern end of the great long, wide street. They took up about one-fifth of the street.

The three-fifths in the middle were taken up by the cattle. The remaining fifth down at the bottom of the town was reserved for the sheep. Pigs were not sold at Castle Island fairs: they had their own weekly market.

Bonhams, however, were sold at all those fairs and they had their own place. It was in about the middle of the town on the southern side, sometimes on the footpath.

There was a good reason for this: young pigs have very

sensitive skins and the nearness of the houses gave them shade from the sun. In the same part of the street, you would see people selling flower plants and infant trees.

Around the same place, you would see the dealers, who were called 'the cash clothes men'. They sold all kinds of garments from the sides of lorries.

You will find in them in that great poem by Robert Burns, 'Tam O'Shanter' – albeit without the lorries:

> *When chapman billies leave the street*
> *And drouthy neighbours neighbours meet . . .*

There too you would meet the men selling a variety of things out of vans: bicycle lamps, leather belts, storm lanterns and all kinds of batteries, not to mention very alarming clocks.

One of the articles that they always had on sale fascinated me because it had so many uses: it had several blades and a corkscrew and a bottle-opener and an instrument for picking grit from horses' hooves.

I was fascinated that the manufacturers in Hong Kong were so well-acquainted with the needs of the Irish peasant.

While all this was going on, the mind games between the jobbers and the sellers provided the texture of the fair. When we were small boys, we hated the big men with the brown boots.

They were taking the calves that we had so lovingly reared up to the midlands, to Longford and Meath and Cavan; to us, they seemed part of a foreign world.

It isn't sentimental to regret the passing of those ancient markets. They were a fundamental part of the economy. They gave fair play to the small man.

He could bargain, down to the last half-crown and beyond. At the fair, he was his own man. In the mart, he has little time for thinking in the presence of the auction-eer's hammer.

The fairs had a cultural value too. They helped to keep alive the old music. It was a November day in Castle Island that I first saw Margaret Barry with her wild banjo slung behind her.

Incidentally, will we ever hear a song called 'She Moved Through the Mart'?

The Pulse of the People

I was born too late and missed out on the great years of journalism. The time was the nineteenth century and the location was the Old West when every settlement had its own paper.

The staff was usually rather small by our standards today: there was the editor and the printer and the lad who ran errands and did the odd jobs.

The equipment in the office was rudimentary: the essentials included a handgun. You may think that it was a Colt .45 or a Smith and Wesson of the same calibre.

I doubt it: they are big and heavy and you need both hands to shoot accurately with them. The gunfighter who is greased lightning on the draw belongs to Hollywood at its most outrageously romantic.

The editors in the Old West preferred a Colt .38. It was usually kept in the drawer on his good side. When he went out for the odd drink, he took with him a derringer. This was a small revolver that fitted easily in your pocket.

It had a short range but this was no handicap in a dispute over a game of poker.

Those intrepid editors in the Old West carried guns in the interest of free speech. When I worked on the *Kerryman*, there were times when I felt like carrying some kind of a gun, preferably a Biretta.

I was the paper's political correspondent: the Northern

Troubles were at their worst; my opinions were not popular with self-styled republicans. A normally decent man travelled from Castle Island to Tralee one day accompanied by six sticks of gelignite.

He intended to put them into the letter box in the front office of the *Kerryman*. For better or worse, it was a church holiday and the office was closed.

Let us speak of happier things. I had great years in that paper. I was my own boss; I could come and go as I liked, provided that the work was done.

In the early days of my time there, the paper's office was located in the living heart of Tralee. It was in a hive of cafés and restaurants and pubs, like Soho in the good old days.

I have long believed that a paper is best located in the middle of life. I would hate to see the *Irish Times* or the *Irish Independent* move out into the country – as they probably will.

When you are in the centre of things, you hear stories, real and imaginary, and jokes, new and antique. Above all, you feel that you are at the hub of the universe.

When the *Kerryman* moved out to an industrial estate east of the town, it took us a long time to adjust. I doubt if my dear friend, Eamon Horan, the brilliant sports writer, ever adjusted at all. He still refers to the new location as 'the Field'.

The *Kerryman* was then – and probably still is – the leading Irish provincial paper. This in loose translation means that it sold the most copies. People bought it for an almost infinite variety of reasons.

Many men bought it for the Football; many women

bought it for the section that told them about the buying and selling of turkeys and ducks and geese and hens. And almost everybody looked to it for its covering of the local courts.

They delighted in reading about some neighbour who had been hauled up for having no light on his bike, or better still, for being drunk and disorderly. The greatest pleasure of all came from reading about the unfortunate who had been apprehended in a pub after hours.

Being a 'found on' gave your neighbours great glee, not because you had committed a heinous crime but because you had been caught.

Gaelic Football was, of course, a big part of the *Kerryman*'s staple diet. It is still, but Soccer is now liberally covered.

In the old days, the alleged catch-and-kick game had a monopoly. If Soccer had even been mentioned, some people would have taken to the streets.

Paddy Foley, God be good to him, was a power in the county's Football in those innocent times. He was the editor of the *Kerryman*; he was its Football correspondent; for great measure, he was for many years a county selector.

His byline consisted simply of his initials; it was hardly a disguise. There may have been a few people in Kerry who had doubts about the Pope's infallibility in the question of faith and morals; fewer still doubted Paddy Foley on Gaelic Football.

Of course he was writing long before television made everybody an expert. Nevertheless, people who had watched Kerry in Croke Park on a Sunday waited eagerly for Paddy's report on the Friday.

He wasn't without a smidgen of prejudice; it might be better to call it chauvinism. He was a man of his age. He was always quick to refute any criticism of Kerry. He excelled himself in the context of the 1939 All-Ireland semi-final between Mayo and ourselves.

The first meeting ended in a draw; it was generally agreed that Mayo had been desperately unlucky, not least because a crucial refereeing decision had gone against them. In the rather bitter aftermath, a spokesman for the Green-Above-The-Red said that Mayo was the best team of all time.

Paddy Foley was not found wanting: he invoked the famous story about the three tailors who arrived together as immigrants in London. They set up shop in the Mile End Road. One advertised himself as the best tailor in the world; another modestly claimed to be the best tailor in London; the third said he was the best tailor in the Mile End Road.

No doubt Paddy was pleased with himself when Kerry ran away with the replay.

The good man was not without hobby horses. One revolved around the pick-up in Football. In those days in Kerry it was almost a mortal sin to pick up the ball without lifting it clearly with the foot.

Elsewhere, it wasn't uncommon to see players picking up the ball with the hands and then giving it a touch with the foot. Paddy Foley labelled this 'the Leinster pick-up'. Today you could call it the All-Ireland pick-up.

His other hobby horse was based on the belief that Kerry were treated unfairly in the context of the championship. His argument appeared simple: because Kerry had no real opposition in Munster, they were at a disadvantage in the

All-Ireland semi-final. He ignored the fact that every county sets out in the All-Ireland without a previous game.

Life went on, and the *Kerryman* sold well. Every Saturday morning in Castle Island Post Office you could see a pile of its copies neatly wrapped and addressed. Many were posted to New York or Boston or Chicago. More went to London or Birmingham or Huddersfield or Luton or Coventry.

Now you can buy the *Kerryman* in the US or Britain within a day or two of its publication. Air freight has changed the world.

On a Sunday recently in Times Square in New York, a friend of mine went to buy the *Kerryman*. The big brown-skinned man at the news-stand said: 'Do you want the Thursday or the Friday edition?'

You can be sure that our people abroad always turn to the notes from their own parish. Those notes keep you in touch with the social life of your heartland. You will be sad to see that a much-loved neighbour has passed away and glad that a local couple have joined in wedlock.

They may have gone back home immediately after the wedding but invariably you will be told that they are spending the honeymoon in the west of Ireland. You will get a tiny arrow of nostalgia when you read the small advertisements.

Your old neighbour, Molly O'Connor, has pullets to sell – White Wyandottes or Black Anconis or maybe Rhode Island Reds.

Denis Walsh, with whom you worked many a day, is selling a young working horse 'guaranteed fair and free'. Tom Brosnan has turnips for sale 'or will exchange for hard black turf'.

Those notes from around the county can give people deeper insights than sociologists or historians.

I think especially of an item from the Knocknagoshel notes, written by my old friend Ned Joe Walsh.

'Eileen and Mary O'Connor, daughters of publican Dan C. D. O'Connor, emigrated to Leeds last Monday. The village will not be the same again.' He never spoke a truer word.

Bogged Down

About four miles north of the town of Castle Island, the ground rises sharply; beyond the horizon is the territory called the Mountain.

It isn't an apt name: it is little more than a thousand feet above the Atlantic and is mostly moorland.

People in the town were hardly aware of it until World War Two cut off the supply of coal from abroad. Suddenly turf was king – and many a man who associated the word with the running of thoroughbred horses came to know the Mountain at first hand.

Some came to hate it; some became obsessed with it. There was no middle way.

Friends of mine who served in the North African desert in the war fell in love with that vastness of sand; the Mountain had much the same effect on people.

Although it was only a few miles from the world down below, it had an atmosphere all of its own. It recalled what D.H. Lawrence said about the messages that rise from the depths of the earth.

The cutting and harvesting of turf isn't always easy; in a bad Summer it can be an exercise in frustration. When Britain was fighting desperately for survival in the early 1940s, the conversation in our local pubs was dominated by the bog.

It was easy to understand this: the Mountain had given

a new dimension to people's lives; it brought them back to their primal selves.

They cooked and ate in the open – and they were as aware of the weather as the animals and the birds.

Thomas Mann, in his novel *The Magic Mountain*, said that if you love a particular activity, you become good at it. He was right.

Some men, who were unaware of the Mountain until they were forced to cut turf for themselves, quickly acquired the skills. Some didn't. The aficionados – those who loved the bog – became as expert as the mountain men.

The skills were only a part of the campaign. There was also the question of knowledge – or, if you like, bog wisdom. You had to know when your turf was fit to foot and when it was fit to stook and when it was fit to draw out.

The weather played a big part: you might postpone the footing or the stocking or the drawing out for a day or two, and then came the rain.

The newcomers took time to acquire this wisdom but some eventually became at least as wise as the native bogmen. Some became even wiser because they weren't inhibited by traditional views.

When your turf was out by the side of the road, you had to build a rick that would keep out the rain. That was a task that called for wisdom. The turf in those days was brought home by horse and cart. The rick could be months in the Mountain.

If your rick wasn't properly built, it would let in the rain and your work would be ruined. When you knew that your rick was soundly constructed, you looked at it like an artist admiring one of his paintings.

You had won the battle. A friend of mine used to say: 'You must fight the bog.' I knew what he meant. I loved the bog, perhaps most of all in the Spring. Then the flowering currant begins to decorate the ditches by the roadside.

It is surprising to see these delicately coloured pink-and-white flowers in a world that seems so hostile to them.

Up in the bog you will see a bird that you wouldn't see inland – the bog lark. When he was going about his business, you didn't need the official weather forecast.

When he left his nest and flew straight upwards, you watched to see how far he would go. If he came down soon, you could expect rain on that day. If he flew so far up that you could no longer see him, you could expect good weather.

There was another good way of forecasting the weather: if the wind or breeze followed the sun, you could be hopeful.

If you had dogs in the bog with you, there was no need of a watch or a clock. They couldn't tell you the time on the first day but they could on the second: at about ten to six, they would wag their tails and begin to look towards home.

The hares too have a good sense of time. If you come to the bog unwontedly early, they will look at you as if saying: 'You shouldn't be here.' And if you remain on beyond the normal time in the evening, you will experience a similar questioning.

The bog hares are not as big as their inland fellows: they have to travel further to eat, they are leaner, and they have more stamina. But they are more vulnerable to bad weather.

I remember especially a day I was in the bog after the

worst spell of weather we ever knew in modern times. The frost and the snow began in January, and the weather didn't really clear until early May; this was in 1947.

On the first morning, I saw a hare sitting upright on the southern side of a stook. He didn't move as I came nearer; I wondered if he happened to be asleep. He was – in the kind of sleep from which he would never awaken. His body was frozen.

Believe it or not, you may see mice in the bog. I saw one for the first time on a day long ago when I was doing a little bit of work with my father and mother.

It was October. We were tidying up some turf that hadn't been dry enough to bring home. As we came near a stook, a mouse came out and moved a short distance away.

She made no attempt to hide; she was acting as a decoy, as some birds, especially the curlew, do. We found her nest in the stook; almost cocooned in it were nine mouselings.

You could fit one of them into a thimble. They were the smallest members of the animal kingdom that we had ever seen. We rearranged the sods as we had found them. The mother mouse soon came back.

I have another especial memory from that same patch of bog. It goes back to a Midsummer Day when my father and myself were drawing out the turf. We expected a day of burning heat and brought two quart bottles of cider to allay the thirst.

I buried them so deep in the bog that if we had forgotten them, they would still be in perfect condition. The day was as hot as we had expected but our drinking was no more than a few mugs of tea at eleven and at one.

Because the bottles were so close to us, we didn't feel

the thirst; we took them home that evening – and consumed them on the premises.

I could fill a big book with stories about the bog, but I will be content with one that I have told many a time in print and in pub.

It concerns a veteran bogman to whom the turf harvest meant a great deal. It was a bad Summer; about the end of August it began to pick up. We felt that if we got another week of sun, all would be well.

On Sunday, as the veteran bogman went into Mass, the sun was shining. The priest of the day was given to long sermons. The bogman soon fell asleep. The good priest paused for effect midway through his sermon.

The silence woke up the veteran. He heard the rain drumming on the roof and said loudly, 'Holy God, bogs are finished.' His words became part of local idiom – and were often invoked to mark calamities far removed from the bog.

Thus when Graham Geraghty scored the goal that ended Kerry's hopes of a comeback in last year's semi-final, I said to myself, 'Bogs are finished.' And so they were.

CÉZANNE
AN EASEL GENIUS

Herbert Read, despite being a native of Yorkshire, became greatly respected as an art critic and a philosopher at large. Nevertheless, he coined the occasional memorable one-liner, such as: 'The past of every reasonable man is strewn with dead enthusiasms.'

It is indeed – and with live enthusiasms too. A long time ago when I was just starting out in secondary school, I was infected with an enthusiasm that seems fated to last the rest of my life.

While reading through a periodical called *The Secondary Book*, I encountered a picture that smote me with an extraordinary sense of wonder.

It was a drawing of a mountain in black and white; from it seemed to emanate a vibrant sense of life – I was entranced. It was the work of a man whose name meant nothing to me but that name became a mantra to brighten many a grey day.

Many years later, when some of his sketches were on exhibition in the Municipal Gallery in Dublin, two of us made the pilgrimage from Kerry in a van that had seen better days. Greater love hath no men.

Paul Cézanne was born in Provence in 1839. His father was that rare being – a liberal banker. He understood his son's decision to quit his law studies and embark on a career as an artist and he saw to it that his son would never lack for money.

Thus Cézanne doesn't fit the popular image of the artist living in an attic and surviving on bread and onions and cheap red wine.

Cézanne was fortunate in another context: in his adolescence he came to know a youth who was as passionate as himself in his ambition to rise above the common world.

Paul Cézanne and Emile Zola walked together and swam together and fished together and dreamed of living in Paris and devoting their lives to fructifying their genius.

A letter from Zola to Cézanne captures the quintessence of youthful dreams.

'For ten years, we have discussed art and literature. We have lived together and often daybreak found us still talking, searching the past and questioning the future.

'We were full of tremendous ideas. We examined and rejected all systems and agreed that, apart from the powerful life of the individual, all else is trivial and worthless.' That letter was written in 1866. Zola was twenty-six; Cézanne was twenty-seven.

Zola was living in Paris; Cézanne was still in Provence. Zola's original ambition was to become a political journalist but he could find no outlet for his ideas – indeed he was scorned.

He turned to drama with a similar lack of success. Cézanne was suffering his own frustrations. When that letter was written, the two friends faced a bleak future. The dreams of young manhood were in dust.

Eventually Zola gained recognition as a novelist; by the time he was thirty-five he was established. Cézanne was still struggling in obscurity. That letter was to have a bitter sequel: Zola published a novel, *L'Oeuvre*, which depicted Cézanne as a heroic failure.

It is impossible to account for this act of betrayal. It couldn't have originated in jealousy or begrudgery. It hurt Cézanne all the more deeply because he knew that it was an honest appraisal. It would be easy to say that time took its revenge on Zola and that his fame was waning as Cézanne's was waxing but it wouldn't be true.

Cézanne's fame came after his death; some of Zola's novels, especially *Germinal* and *L'Assommoir*, read as well today as when they were first published.

How could Zola be so wrong in his judgement of Cézanne's work? If he was prejudiced at all, it was in Cézanne's favour. We must ask a similar question about the loosely associated group called the Impressionists.

The public reaction to the Impressionists' first exhibition was almost hysterical. I cannot help suspecting that this was due not so much to their revolutionary ideas about painting as to their subject matter.

In their paintings, we see laundry women yawning over the ironing board, peasants having a supper that consists of little more than potatoes, and the working people of Paris dancing their cares away.

Cézanne hadn't much sympathy with the working class. He wouldn't have admired the gallant people of Paris who manned and womanned the barricades during the Commune and thus saved the honour of France.

He wasn't around either to disapprove or to admire: he fled from Paris at the advance of the Germans – unlike Samuel Beckett, who, to his eternal credit, chose to live in wartime France rather than return to Ireland.

The second half of the nineteenth century in France – and especially in Paris – was a period of unprecedented ferment in politics, literature and the arts.

The first quarter of the twentieth century in Ireland – and especially in Dublin – could be compared to it but only in a small way.

Cézanne lived in Paris through some of the most exciting years that the capital ever knew but he seems to have been unaffected by events there.

On rare nights, he visited some of those cafés where writers and intellectuals casually came together but he always remained on the fringe of the company and hardly ever spoke. He was hopelessly shy and was in thrall to melancholy, depression and self-doubt, but in the midst of all this suffering there was a terrible core of certainty. He might falter on his path but he knew where he was going.

Henry Moore paid him the ultimate accolade: 'Cézanne battled against all the things that he admired in painting.'

Moore went on: 'I believe that it is better to attempt something you cannot do rather than what comes easy.'

He exhibited on a few occasions with the Impressionists but eventually felt that he had nothing in common with them and nothing to learn from them. Nonetheless, he continued to admire their work, especially that of Edouard Manet and Camille Pissarro.

Cézanne's method of working became legendary: he took so long at painting flowers and fruit that sometimes the flowers became withered and the fruit became wizened.

He and Gerard Manley Hopkins were more or less contemporaries; they were hardly aware of each other but were remarkably alike.

Hopkins lived in Dublin in yeasty years but he seemed to be unaffected by it: he had no sympathy for Irish nationalism; he passed through the city like a ghost and left little trace.

You will find hardly anything of Paris in Cézanne's work; the same is true of Hopkins in relation to Dublin. Both men were outsiders.

Hopkins believed that the language of poetry had become tired, and he laboured to create a new language. Cézanne likewise believed that traditional painting had run its course.

He spent endless hours over what seemed simple themes because he desired to capture what Hopkins called the inscape of things.

'Inscape' is not an easy word to explain: he meant that things should leap at you out of his poetry in a way that you had never known before.

Cézanne cherished that same feeling: he would love to think that he could paint an apple and make you see it with the eye of childhood, as if you had never seen an apple before.

In his later years he returned to the family home and his first love, the countryside of Provence. He wasn't welcomed by his neighbours. They disapproved of the wealthy man who went around dressed like a tramp and painted in the fields in all weathers. He was letting down the side.

Cézanne's terrible core of certainty sustained him. As he grew older, he became more and more obsessed with capturing the essence of his native place and especially that of Mont Sainte-Victoire.

D. H. Lawrence spoke about the messages that came to us from the depths of the earth. It was said that he could describe people in a field and that you would remember the field when you had forgotten the people. Cézanne would have understood.

I understand why the Aborigines of Australia venerate Ayer's Rock and I understand why Cézanne was obsessed with Mont Sainte-Victoire.

Mountains, with their sense of solidity and permanence are like fathers; rivers are like mothers.

Mont Sainte-Victoire is a friendly mountain; its contours are gentle and its slopes have been cultivated for generations. Cézanne strove to capture its spirit. I believe that his drawings and paintings of that mountain are among his greatest works. While painting in the fields in October 1906, Cézanne was caught in a violent rainstorm, and on his way home he collapsed by the roadside.

He was brought back in a laundry van. On the morrow he got up and worked as intensely as ever. He died from pneumonia a week later.

He wasn't without friends in his later days. A little group of local young intellectuals idolised him, possibly as much for his heroism as for his painting. In a way, his life had a happy ending.

Offaly's Glorious First

Since the All-Ireland became a purely inter-county competition sixty years ago, only eight names have appeared on the trophy.

And the latest new name was in 1955 when Wexford at last reaped a harvest.

But it wasn't their first attempt in a final – they had lost narrowly to Cork the year before.

And Galway last year had ended a long drought after they too had suffered defeat in the previous final.

And so Offaly yesterday found themselves facing not only the reigning champions: there was also the old husbands' tale that before being summoned to the round table you must already have been rebuffed at least once.

And the 'traditionalists' – those amusing mystics who believe that it takes several generations to produce a hurler – looked on as Offaly's presence in the final as aficionados of the bullring might look on an Irish matador.

Galway were hoping to make history too – if on a lesser stage.

They had never won the minor title – they were the only members of the round table not to have done so.

It was Offaly's first time being in Croke Park in a Hurling final of any kind.

They won the junior title in 1929 – but the final was

played in Birr. It was on a December Sunday – and only about five hundred watched.

It was hardly a glamorous setting – but Mick Digan remembered it well.

He played on the winning team on that near-Christmas Day long ago – when a pint of stout was eight old pence and a labourer was expected to survive on a little over a pound a week.

Mick, needless to say, is loyal to his generation – and reckons the Hurling was far better in his day. Players now, he says, cannot pull on the overhead ball.

And what does he think of men who like to run with the ball on the hurley? 'They're like a woman feeding hens,' he says. So now . . .

Mick lives snugly in his thatched cottage and didn't travel to Croke Park yesterday; he watched the battle on television.

And he surely reflected on the great changes that have taken place in Hurling and in Ireland since that Winter day long ago when he won his place in the folk gallery.

Another man with cause to reflect on change yesterday was Tom Donoghue, Offaly's full-back.

A year ago he stood on Hill 16 – and watched his native county wash away the bitterness and sadness of two generations.

Tom had played for Galway when they won their Under-21 All-Ireland – but now he was nearing thirty, had drifted away from Hurling into Rugby, and in his wildest daydreams didn't see himself ever again playing in Croke Park on a final day.

Yet yesterday he was little more than an hour from the

highest honour – and it wouldn't be a whit diminished if earned with his adopted county.

His involvement made even more piquant the meeting of these Shannon-divided neighbours.

Another piquant aspect was that while the Offaly players spent Saturday night in their own beds, a big advance guard of their supporters invaded Dublin on the eve of the battle.

It was as if they felt their early presence might be a blow in the psychological welfare, a little source of unease to Galway and their followers, who came as usual on the Saturday.

And by noon yesterday there were so many Offaly people in Dublin that you hoped no cow in the Faithful County would slip into a drain or no ass wander into a bog-hole.

And you feared that if the Martians landed there, not even the gallant Mick Digan would be able to do much about it.

The county of Galway was just as vulnerable: by half past one when their minors came out to do battle with Kilkenny, the Maroon-and-White was blossoming all over Croke Park.

Seldom can the headquarters have been so well populated so early. Even then there were big queues outside the Canal Terrace, an almost-forgotten sight at a Hurling final.

And the Maroon-and-White forest waved in the very first minute as a flashing goal gave Galway the kind of start that helped their seniors topple Cork in that unforgettable semi-final of '75.

But Kilkenny showed the coolness that seems part of their heritage – and it was soon clear that this was to be a struggle that would continue all the way into the home straight.

Galway seemed the better in the first half – but the light wind blowing into the Canal goal was probably a factor in their apparent superiority.

The teams were level going into the last quarter – and for about six minutes there was a fierce battle of nerves as both strove to pull clear.

Galway were the more dashing – but Kilkenny the more crafty. And in the last furlong they stole away in the fashion long associated with the Black and Amber.

It was the old Kilkenny formula: look for the points – and let the goals look for themselves.

The points came in a little stream – and you felt that 'Flow on Lovely River' could be equally applied to Hurling.

At the end it was 1–20 to 3–9 – and Galway were still without a minor title.

The setback didn't seem to worry their huge following – and there was a carnival air as the champions ran out a few minutes before three.

The biggest Maroon-and-White banner at the Canal End said with mock politeness, 'We're Offaly Sorry'.

The banter in the crowd was friendly – and there was about as much danger of violence on the terraces as of a shower of snow.

Despite the wind, the terrace crowds were sweltering – and the ice-cream vendors would have been set up for life if only they could devise a method of delivering their merchandise from overhead.

The green pitch looked like an oasis – and you envied the players their freedom of movement.

It is doubtful if many of them looked up to see the colour of the sky: it was dry-blue and the sun shone brightly into the eyes of those behind the Railway goal.

The march provoked such an orgy of flags and banners that you feared a clothing shortage; the National Anthem was guillotined by a hurricane of sound.

It came as a blessed relief when Frank Murphy loosed the ball – at last the mill of the mind could grind on something substantial.

It eased the tension in the crowd – but the men on the field were obviously not as confident as their followers.

And there was thirty seconds of stuttering and stammering before Ger Coughlan uttered the first long sentence.

It led to a free for his side – and Pat Delaney rifled over an eighty-yard point with the coolness of William Tell.

Michael Conneely's puck-out indicated the help given by the wind – and brought a Galway surge and a low shot from Joe Connolly.

Damian Martin held it cleanly – but then went on a too-ambitious run that brought Galway a free. Joe Connolly lofted it over – the battle was truly on.

As the players settled, the Hurling began to glow – and now we saw Offaly's fierce determination and Galway's menacing fluency.

In that trying time for Offaly as they faced the champions and the wind, their hero was Ger Coughlan.

The little left half-back was playing as if he had the power of seeing the future: time and again he put his hurley in the hole in the dyke-wall.

His namesake Eugene at full-back was doing well too – and even though the corner-backs, Tom Donoghue and Pat Fleury, were struggling, they were giving little away.

But outfield, Galway were playing majestically – as if

determined not only to win but to silence forever those who doubted their standing.

Seldom has Croke Park seen such magnificent points as flowed over the Canal goal.

Whenever a Galway man shot, the ball seemed like a homing pigeon.

Only one thing marred this great first half: you had to pity the referee as he tried to chase away the bottle-carriers and the counsellors and the bone-setters and the physiologists and the next of kin and the sympathisers and the motivators.

There was a major hold-up in the tenth minute – and when play restarted, Johnny Flaherty made a little run and set up Pat Carroll for a great drive from thirty yards that went to the net off an upright.

Offaly now led 1–2 to 0–3.

By the mid-point of the half, the westerners were back in front, 0–6 to 1–2. And Steve Mahon was growing to such stature that Offaly were almost eclipsed in midfield.

In the eighteenth minute he decorated his work with a mighty point.

In the twentieth minute Finbar Gantley rattled the bar above Damian Martin's head; the ball flew wide.

The puck-out was returned – Joe Connolly was playing superbly and sent over another glorious point.

Two minutes later John Connolly set the western crowd roaring as he went charging through.

As he came into the small rectangle, he collided with Damian Martin. The ball ended up in the net – but a free-out was signalled.

It hardly seemed to matter at the time – Galway were

rampant. But it figured large in the pub enquiry.

Pat Delaney eased Offaly's pain with another great point from a free. Michael Connolly answered with an even better point from play.

In the twenty-seventh minute Liam Currans at last showed a flash of his talent with a lovely lift-and-strike that brought a point. Noel Lane made a darting run and replied.

Galway seemed to abound in confidence – and Joe Connolly especially looked infallible.

At the other end of the field Niall McInerney was cleaning up like a sheriff in an outrageously romantic western.

Galway's half-time lead – 0–13 to 1–4 – seemed no more than their due. And if anyone tells you he foresaw the second half, he is either a liar or a prophet.

It is true that the wind was a factor – but it hardly accounts for the change that came over Galway.

If this had happened in the days of the Borgias, you would have suspected that someone had interfered with their interval drink.

But in the third quarter – with Mahon still outstanding – they won as much of the ball as before.

But now the homing pigeons behaved as if a cat was in the loft.

They stayed out – and as Galway's forwards lost their touch, they attempted to take the ball close in and go for goals.

At the other end Paddy Horan showed more sense. Despite Galway's big lead, he was content to take a point from a twenty-one-yard free.

Yet Galway seemed in no great danger – and at the mid-point of the half led 0–15 to 1–8. And their followers awaited the killing surge.

It never came. Galway, in fact, had got their last score. The shots for points continued to go wide – and the few that were accurate and low brought out the best in Damian Martin.

But Offaly's attackers were doing little better. The ball was not running kindly for Paddy Horan and Johnny Flaherty – and Pat Carroll was the most likely rainmaker.

But in looking back you could clearly see the part played by Offaly's half-forwards. Pat Kirwan and Brendan Birmingham and Mark Corrigan were not spectacular but they held down Galway's great half-back line.

And now in the final quarter Joachim Kelly and Liam Currams began to flower in midfield. Behind them was the lion-hearted Delaney.

Joe Connelly had inflicted a harrowing first half on him – and he had been glad of the cover given by Aidan Fogarty and Ger Coughlan.

But he never lost head or heart – and his resurgence was a symbol of Offaly's sheer grit.

In the twenty-fifth minute he scored a lovely point from play – it seemed to give Offaly the scent of victory.

Then Iggy Clarke wided a seventy. Galway seemed becalmed.

And then at last we saw a drop of the purest Flaherty – a sweet point made the score 0–15 to 1–10. Five minutes remained.

And there was more Flaherty to come. Less than two minutes later Delaney, Kelly and Birmingham combined to put the Offaly rover through.

And from the razor's edge of the small rectangle he served up a triple-drop by palming to the net. All heaven broke loose – and its colours were green, white and gold.

Then Danny Owens – who like Brendan Keeshan came on as a second-half sub – hit a thundering point. Offaly were two up. Both subs excelled.

Then Horan from a free made the final score 2–12 to 0–15. But I doubt if most of the Offaly crowd knew it exactly – they were gone out of their delighted minds.

And Tom Donoghue was marvelling at how his fortune had changed since a year ago he paid £2 into the Hill.

And a deputation from Kinnity were holding down Johnny Flaherty lest he be taken away into the heavens in a fiery chariot.

And back at home in his snug thatched cottage Mick Digan was saying to himself that the fire he had fomented was now a blazing beacon.

Evening Press, September 1981

John Clare
The Lost Child of Nature

John Clare is probably the greatest of England's half-forgotten poets. He was born in 1793 but his bicentenary went almost unnoticed.

He was a native of what is surely the most hidden part of England – the flat land of which Peterborough is the spiritual capital.

Eels love slow-moving water; Ely is 'the Island of the Eels'; it symbolises the nature of that quiet world.

It isn't far from the sea and yet it seems to be quint-essentially midland.

Clare was born into as working-class a family as you could find: his father was a farm labourer and his mother was no stranger to the fields.

Because he was a genius – if that much-abused word has any meaning at all – doubts were cast on his parentage.

Legend tells us that his father was a member of the travelling class – an Irishman who was an itinerant fiddle player.

The probable truth is rather more prosaic: Clare's contemporaries could hardly credit that he was the son of 'ordinary' people.

He had much in common with Francis Ledwidge; his father too was a farm labourer, and his mother had to work in the fields when she was widowed.

Both Clare and Ledwidge knew the trauma of falling in

love with someone who was hopelessly out of reach because of the social divide.

War brought Ledwidge's life to an early close; insanity seemed to have ended Clare's output as a poet.

That is the general image of him, if there is any image at all.

Clare entered an asylum when he was young but he continued to produce rivers of poetry.

It is doubtful if he was ever insane; R. D. Laing might have said that he was too sane to cope with a mad world.

Clare's parents resembled Ledwidge's in that they appreciated their son's gift and gave him all the help and encouragement that they could.

A local lord helped to get his first book published.

It was widely acclaimed and went into several editions; his fame, alas, waned as quickly as it had waxed.

He had to support a wife and family. She was wont to use his manuscripts to light the fire; this was taking literary criticism rather far.

Never was a man more a child of the fields and the woods and the streams.

We are all to some degree influenced by our surroundings; it is fair to say that Clare was moulded by his.

The countryside that he knew so intimately and loved so passionately survives now in fragments.

The enclosure of the commons was the first blow; mechanised farming struck the second; the coming of the motorways was the third.

Strangely enough, the advent of the railway, though it brought enormous social change, did little to alter the rural tegument.

Indeed, in one sense it enhanced it; in the embankments you will find wild flowers that elsewhere have become extinct.

Clare loved 'the secret places': copses and woods and marshes that probably only he appreciated.

He would have understood Patrick Kavanagh's 'undying difference in the corner of a field'.

He knew flowers as yet 'unchristened'.

In that too he resembles Kavanagh:

> *The burnet*
> *saxifrage was there*
> *in profusion*
> *And the autumn*
> *gentian. I knew*
> *them all by eyesight long before*
> *I knew their names.*
> *We were in love*
> *before we were*
> *introduced.*

The enclosure of the common land robbed Clare of his birthright.

It was a cynical act; the pretext was that 'rationalisation' would greatly improve agricultural produce, but the real reason was sheer greed.

Hedges were levelled; copses were cut down; marshes were drained. It was as if a great wild river had been canalised.

Clare fell into a depression; the bright young man became melancholy to the point of despair.

When he entered the asylum, it was as if saying, 'I will not serve.' He wanted no part of the new world.

He admired his contemporary, John Keats, but no two could have been more different in their concept of poetry.

Keats was embedded in the English lyrical tradition; Clare went his own way.

I have long believed that poets are the makers of language.

In the early days of man's most precious gift, a great many things were 'unchristened'.

Someone minted names; the community endorsed his findings.

In Clare's poetry you will find words that he seems to have invented.

And he didn't hesitate to adapt an existing word: thus we find him talking of 'the roundy sun'.

And this is how he sees a fish that few would deem worthy of a place in poetry:

> The gudgeons
> sturting bye
> Cringd neath grasses'
> shade
> Startling as each
> nimble eye
> Saw the rings to droppies made.

Those few lines are the quintessence of John Clare; his genius resides in his awareness of an almost-hidden world and his ability to express it consummately.

His was the most original voice in English poetry until

the arrival of Gerard Manley Hopkins.

Only he could talk of the cuckoo's 'pleasant rustling noise' and the heron 'cranking a jarring melancholy cry' and coin words such as 'mooring', 'drippling' and 'brustling'.

Clare was so enthralled by the countryside of his youth that he felt lost when only a few miles away from it.

'The very wild flowers seemed to forget me and I imagined they were the inhabitants of a new country; the very sun seemed to be a new one and slung in a different corner of the sky.'

You can understand his disorientation when he found himself in a mental home in Essex: no countryside in England could be more different from his own.

After four years, he did a runner and walked the many miles back home – only it was no longer home because so much of his heartland had been destroyed.

His wife, a good country girl called Patty, did all she could for him – but in vain.

He was admitted to Northampton asylum and spent the rest of his days there. He died in 1864; he was seventy-one.

If anything can be certain in the field of mental health, it is that the enclosure devastated John Clare.

He was a child of the old feudal England. Feudalism wasn't all bad: a good landlord was the protector of the peasants.

Greed replaced benevolence in the new order; the old bonds were disrupted; Clare thought of himself as a superfluous man.

His best-known poem is a terrible cry from the heart:

I am! yet what I am who cares, or knows?
        My friends forsake me like a memory lost.
I am the self-consumer of my woes;
        They rise and vanish, an oblivious host,
Shadows of life, whose very soul is lost.
And yet I am – I live – though I am toss'd

Into the nothingness of scorn and noise,
        Into the living sea of waking dream,
Where there is neither sense of life, nor joys,
        But the huge shipwreck of my own esteem
And all that's dear. Even those I loved the best
Are strange – nay, they are stranger than the rest.

I long for scenes where man has never trod –
        For scenes where woman never smiled or wept –
There to abide with my Creator, God,
        And sleep as I in childhood sweetly slept,
Full of high thoughts, unborn. So let me lie –
The grass below; above, the vaulted sky.

                    Evening Press, 22 September 1993

58

The Glory Days Return for Kerry

It was all so different when I lived in Kerry. Whoever said that absence makes the heart grow fonder was spot on; I realised the truth of this one-liner in the run-up to the All-Ireland final of 1975. For better or worse, I was then living in Dublin. The game took on a deeper emotional involvement for me than when I was living down at home.

On the morning of the battle I didn't partake of a hearty breakfast – indeed I hadn't a breakfast at all. It was a strange occasion: for once Kerry were the outsiders; they had a very young, untested team – you could back them at 5 to 4. Dublin were reigning champions and had performed so well on the way to the title that there was enormous confidence behind them.

A colleague of mine who was a printer in Burgh Quay lost the run of himself on the Saturday night at Shelbourne Park – he put the holiday money on Dublin; in the aftermath his wife wasn't too pleased. They wouldn't be going to the sun; they spent the holidays in Donabate. A wicked colleague said: 'It wasn't the Canaries, it was the Seagulls.'

I have very vivid memories of the prologue to the All-Ireland final of 1978. Dublin were even stronger favourites than in 1975. It made sense: they had beaten Kerry convincingly in the final in 1976 and more so in the semi-final in 1977.

We were very apprehensive. About five o'clock on the Friday evening before the game, the bell rang in my house; outside there was a great friend of mine with his little post-office van – what was surely the shortest conversation of all time took place.

Frank Wynne, who has long since departed this world, said, 'Well . . . ' and I said, 'We'll win.' He got into his van and drove away – I was embarrassed that he had such faith in me; well, we won.

At the risk of being barred from my native county, I will argue that Kerry had luck riding shotgun for them on this year's voyage to Autumn Gold.

We didn't encounter the forces we feared most: Clare took out Cork; Cavan eliminated Derry; Meath put out Dublin and were in turn knocked out by Offaly. We didn't fear Mayo because we believed that they were spiritually exhausted; we were wrong there.

Now let us look at the semi-final. Don't tell me that we beat Cavan easily. It's fine to boast that you hadn't feared the storm when you are safe in port. I didn't breathe easily until Miko Russell's goal a few minutes from the end.

About five minutes before, I was convinced that Cavan should have had a penalty; if converted, it would have put them ahead – and only the gods could tell what would happen after that.

The late stages of the final were remarkably similar: we were hanging on by the proverbial thread until Maurice Fitzgerald launched that great point from his hands in the sixty-ninth minute – then I knew that we would get at least a draw.

I didn't celebrate that night: I was more relieved than

overjoyed – and I remembered a story told by the late John Rafferty, the great sportswriter who doubled as a Boxing manager.

His greatest moment came when Jackie Paterson won the World Flyweight Championship. There was only one version of the title then – it was a great achievement. John had guided Jackie from boyhood; it was a night of wild celebration in Glasgow.

What did John do after the fight? He went straight home to bed.

Many people have argued that this year's final was mediocre; I couldn't agree less. The texture was uneven: it was a patchwork quilt of a game that contained many bright colours. Above all, it was sporting: 'And for this relief, much thanks.' For once, a final left little room for controversy.

It will be remembered as Maurice Fitzgerald's final; he had been so long playing with Kerry that we had almost forgotten it was his first. He had often been accused of underperforming but he certainly picked the right day to display all his talents.

There was a belief down in Kerry that Maurice would never win an All-Ireland medal – and as time went by, that belief grew; it was especially strong after last year's semi-final.

The litany of great players who didn't win gold is very impressive and rather sad: it includes two Kerrymen, Eddie Dowling and my friend Denis O'Sullivan – they just came along at the wrong time. Count in Gerry O'Malley and Packie McGarty and Moses Coffey. Moses was hardly known outside Wicklow but, believe me, he was cast in a hectic mould.

The gods may have smiled on Kerry on their way to winning the All-Ireland but there can be no question about their all-round supremacy in 1997 – they won the League in brilliant style.

The final of that fairer competition provided me with the best day in the sporting year: I was down at the fence behind the City goal about halfway between the posts and the right-hand corner flag. Now read on . . .

It was raining heavily but I didn't mind: by the fiftieth minute I knew that Kerry were going to win; the rest of the game was like a lap of honour – I was as happy as a child in sand.

Dylan Thomas
From Monster to Magician

When he departed from this mortal world a little over forty years ago, his local paper devoted only a few paragraphs to his passing; the 'big' papers in these islands gave him ample space and fulsome praise.

Laugharne, the little town in south-west Wales where he spent much of his adult life, is now a place of pilgrimage; Dylan Thomas is an icon.

He is also an immortal, if that word has any meaning at all; Thomas was a monster but he was also a great poet.

The surface events of his life have been intimately chronicled; to call him immoral or amoral would be woefully inadequate.

He had a heroic ambition to avoid what is conventionally known as work; to get by he begged and 'borrowed' and stole and sponged; there was usually some silly woman ready to lavish money on him.

His wife, Caitlin, was little better; they were a couple whom you wouldn't invite home to meet your mother even if you were certain that she was out.

Her life, unlike his, was tragic; she was fiercely ambitious to make her way in the world of the arts but failed abysmally.

She set out as a dancer in the mode of Isadora Duncan but never got beyond the chorus in Charles Cochrane's revues.

As a painter, she never got beyond the stage of dabbling.

Ironically, she had a talent for writing but was too inhibited to exercise it while Dylan was alive.

She lived in his shadow even after his death.

If you are unfortunate enough to have read all that has been written about Thomas, you will feel that you know his every move from the cradle to the grave.

This kind of semi-voyeurism doesn't of course tell you what made him a poet; it is little more than gossip for middlebrows.

There can, however, be no doubt about one factor in his conditioning: his mother spoiled him outrageously.

Nothing in her scheme of things was good enough for him; in her eyes, he could do no wrong.

Thomas Wolfe too had an adoring mother and he too was a monster – an ingrate who trampled on his friends, all the more so if they happened to be women.

And he shared with Thomas Hardy a trait common to most bohemians: an obsession with money.

You can invoke Thomas Hardy to complete an unholy trinity: he was another mother's boy who grew up to be a cold and miserly man.

There is a parallel between Hardy's wife, Emma, and Caitlin Thomas; Emma Hardy too was ambitious to be a writer but despaired in the light of her husband's fame.

If there is a moral in all this, it is that some artists are so driven by their ambition that they are blind to all human considerations.

And inherent in this truth, if truth it be, there is an enormous paradox: Thomas and Wolfe and Hardy were cruelly insensitive to people in what we call the real world and yet marvellously sensitive in their writing.

Perhaps there is another moral in the story of those three men who were so spoiled by their mothers: they started out in life with unbounded confidence.

Thomas was a published poet at twenty; Hardy's first novel was the work of a young man who was determined to break from convention; Wolfe owed nothing to those American writers who were deemed the giants of the nineteenth century.

Thomas may have owed more to tradition than Hardy and Wolfe, albeit in a negative way. Consciously or otherwise, he rebelled against the kind of poetry that was influenced by Eliot and Auden. And in doing so, he harked back to another world – the English lyrical tradition.

That seemed to have reached its crest with Tennyson; it is hard not to suspect that Gerard Manley Hopkins broke away from it deliberately – because he so revered it.

And it is hard to resist drawing a parallel between the poetry of Hopkins and the Impressionist movement in painting.

Hopkins grew up in what you might call a classical period in English poetry.

Herbert Read looked at the term 'Romantic' as essentially an awareness that a certain tradition had reached its fulfilment.

The Impressionists were saturated with the work of the Old Masters; they revered them but felt the need for a new mode.

You feel the same sense of quiet revolution in Hopkins; his poetry is in the lyrical tradition but is innovative in technique.

He broke away from conventional prosody and syntax; he delighted in minting words that were all his own.

If his work had been published in his lifetime, he would almost certainly have encountered critical hostility – as the Impressionists did.

Dylan Thomas was critically accepted from the start; his work was like warm rain on a field that had been too long fallow.

John Donne would have relished his bold imagery, even if some of it is unsuccessful.

Some of the articles devoted to the fortieth anniversary of Dylan's death put too much stress on the surface of his life.

We met the foul-mouthed, bibulous buffoon – the man who seemed to spend most of his life in pubs or other places of low resort.

These facts – if facts they be – disguise his essential nature: he was a poet who took his craft as seriously as Hopkins or Tennyson or any of his other great predecessors.

He reached his Everest with 'Fern Hill' – in it all his talents most happily come together.

It was to him as 'The Elegy' was to Gray, 'The Immortality Ode' was to Wordsworth, 'The Skylark' was to Shelley, and 'The Wreck of the Deutschland' was to Hopkins.

It is a classic, if that words means an impulse consummately expressed.

Thomas had a kinship with D. H. Lawrence; both lived for part of their lives in a land where the Industrial Revolution grew up amid the fields.

Lawrence was a son of the Nottingham coalfield; he was never far from the country; his awareness of one world heightened his awareness of the other.

It was much the same with Thomas: 'Fern Hill' is the hymn of a city child enthralled by Swansea's rural hinterland.

Dylan was part of an extended family. Aren't all the people of Wales?

As a child, he spent holidays with his mother's parents on a small farm – and discovered an enchanting world:

> *Now I was young and easy under the apple boughs.*
> *About the lilting house and happy as the grass was*
> > *green . . .*
> *And I was green and carefree, famous among the barns*
> *About the happy yard and singing as the farm was*
> > *home . . .*
> *All the sun long it was running, it was lovely, the hay*
> *Fields high as the house . . .*
> *Nothing I cared in the lamb white days, that time would*
> > *take me*
> *Up to the swallow thronged loft by the shadow of my*
> > *hand.*
> *Time held me green and dying*
> *Though I sang in my chains like the sea.*

Evening Press, 15 December 1993

Hurling's Hoary Myth is Dead

I wasn't in Dublin on the eve of Clontarf and I haven't an inkling of the mood on that day; perhaps the atmosphere was little different from the usual.

Perhaps the fishermen down below in Ringsend were following the ancient profession adorned by Peter and his brethren and perhaps Molly's ancestors were busier than usual because a day of abstinence was imminent – all I know is that the peasants of Brabant milked their cows on the morning of Waterloo.

I suppose it is fair to say that this afternoon's showdown is awaited as eagerly as any Hurling All-Ireland ever; it isn't too long since you could stroll up to Croke Park after the pubs closed and be sure of getting in to one terrace or the other.

The attendance at the final between Galway and Kilkenny in 1975 was under 54,000. Whence has come the revolution – if it is really a revolution.

The underlying cause may be simple: in the last quarter of a century we have seen a hoary myth shattered beyond repair. All the mumblings of the traditionalists cannot put back it together again but of course we still have to suffer the old husbands' tales about how great the game was long ago.

I am old enough to remember when the keeper was fair (foul) game for the hitmen and when the famous dust rising from the goalmouths in Thurles didn't always some from strokes aimed at the *sliotar*.

The good old days are here now. The old husbands will tell you that such arts as the double are no more. Gerald McCarthy seems assured of his place in folklore as its last great exponent.

The extra velocity of the new ball has made the double much more difficult to achieve. It has also of course changed the tactics of the game: most keepers now can drop the puck-out to within forty yards of goal – indeed with the help of the wind they can trouble their counterparts.

I need hardly add that we have seen great Hurling in the Leinster and Munster championships this season. At least six games have whetted the appetites – and the semi-finals did nothing to unwhet them.

Galway and Wexford produced a splendid game. Limerick fell below expectations but to me it seemed that for the first time in their history we saw Antrim progress from being pretenders to becoming contenders.

The long absence of Limerick and Wexford from the crock of gold under the rainbow has added to the ferment.

A fair proportion of the lads and lassies whose hearts will rise and sink and rise this afternoon have never known their counties win September glory.

To me it seems only a few years ago since Limerick took gold – in fact, twenty-three years have gone by; Wexford haven't been in the winners' enclosure since 1968.

The people who will most create the atmosphere today are not the players or the younger followers but the veteran aficionados, man and women who have suffered so many false springs and so many broken harvests – they are not so much hungry as ravenous.

They yearn to walk down Fitzgibbon Street like a

conquering army. I should be more excited about today's game than about any Hurling final ever because both forces are dear to my heart. I need hardly add that in our part of Kerry we follow the green and white.

Indeed there were times when I grieved for Limerick more than for Kerry because I was confident that our absence from Croke Park would be short. Alas . . .

I grieved especially after the All-Ireland semi-final between Galway and Limerick in 1981. That was the occasion when Sean Foley was very harshly sent off.

Sean wrote me a long letter about his trauma: he felt that his dismissal had cost Limerick the game and probably the All-Ireland. I never showed that letter to anybody – Sean's sorrow was intensely private.

Limerick folk will tell you that the tragic loss of that semi-final cast a gloom from which it has taken a long time to recover.

My admiration for the hurlers of Wexford and their followers is hardly a secret: on their great days they seem to elevate the ancient craft onto a new plateau.

I am thinking especially about the Leinster final of 1976. On that astonishing occasion they devastated Kilkenny with an art that seemed to have been invented by the black and amber; we saw points flying home like arrows from the bow of William Tell.

If asked to name my favourite person in Irish sport, Tony Doran would be a warm contender: he had a quality that was hard to define but easy to recognise. I will content myself by describing that quality as heroic.

He always seemed to be striving to go beyond his limits; the spirit seemed as important as his range of skills.

When I invoke the term 'heroic', I think of Mick Mackey and Tom Cheasty and Pat Hartigan and George O'Connor. You may wonder why I didn't mention Ring: Christy achieved his great deeds by his superb skills.

The maestro from Cloyne rarely did anything that surprised you but he did the fundamental things so well that he was very hard to counter.

The heroic isn't altogether past tense: Mick Houlihan and Ciaran Carey have a touch of it – so has Martin Storey. They could be the stars of this enthralling battle but the gods have a tendency to write disquieting scenarios.

Thus sometimes the bit players shine while the stars are dimmed. I must confess that there was a showdown in Hurling to which I looked forward with even greater anticipation than I do to that of this afternoon.

It was arranged for a Sunday afternoon in the 1860s and I was twelve years of age. Lovers of Charles Kickham and his great book *Knockagow* need no telling. The teams were to be the farmers and the farmers' boys. It threatened to be class warfare.

The game wasn't all-ticket but there was a great crowd in the Field. Twenty-one good men and true would do battle for their tribes.

Mat Donovan, I need hardly add, was captain of the labourers. 'There was a hush and an anxious look on many a face as he strode towards the middle of the field', and 'Some of the players were quite pale and their teeth were chattering with excitement.'

Mat is puzzled when he sees that the opposition are not taking their places. The explanation is soon forthcoming: their captain, Tom Cuddehy, is missing.

A young lad comes running and says, 'Ould Paddy Loughlan's daughter is after running away with him.' The farmers wouldn't play without him and so it is agreed to play a mixed match.

I never forgave Paddy Loughlan's daughter – she almost turned me against the feminine gender for life. It is most unlikely that some oul' lad's daughter will run off with Ciaran Carey or Martin Storey before the throw-in this afternoon.

The captains, incidentally, were rather more important in the old days. Sometimes they acted as dual referees. Could you imagine that happening now?

By this morning every aspect of every player involved this afternoon has been parsed and analysed and all the anticipated duels have been scrutinised. The truth of course is that many of these duels never materialise.

Hurling, far more than Gaelic Football or Soccer or Rugby, is tantalisingly unpredictable.

When I make a forecast about the outcome of a game in those three, I have comparatively solid reasons.

When you make a prediction about a Hurling game in which the teams seem to be evenly matched, you are whistling past your obituary as a pundit.

To argue that Hurling is akin to Cricket may seem a wild statement – but think about it . . .

The ball in both is about the same size; at times they can travel at about a hundred miles an hour and can behave wickedly both in the air and off the pitch.

In the context of Gaelic Football, Soccer and Rugby, you are often dealing with inches; in Hurling and Cricket you are sometimes dealing in centimetres.

A tiny edge off the bat can cost a wicket; a similar edge off the *camán* can make or save a goal.

Sometimes I suspect that the gremlins reserve their most insidious tricks for All-Ireland Hurling finals and they never seem to have any difficulty getting tickets.

They seem to take an especial delight in tormenting keepers. When I saw Michael Walsh giving away a goal in an All-Ireland final, I knew then that no keeper was invulnerable.

Joe Quaid and Damien Fitzhenry have been in splendid form all season. Limerick's keeper may seem to have an advantage because he has already played in a final but his counterpart is more familiar with Croke Park.

Those Wexford people who believe in omens may take heart from the fact that Liam Griffin owns a string of hotels; so does Brian McEniff, who led Donegal in their year of glory.

How can I make a forecast? My heart says Limerick. My head says Wexford. My head is in confusion. I have seen Limerick only once this season – that is, apart from on television. I have seen Wexford three times – they excelled against Offaly and Galway.

I have no doubts about Limerick's defenders and mid-fielders. Unless their forwards make a great leap upward, my neighbours in the hills north of Castle Island will not see the glow from the bonfires in Abbeyfeale and Broadford and Templeglantine and Castlemahon and beyond.

I need hardly add that the hoary myth is the belief that Cork, Tipperary and Kilkenny are Hurling's aristocrats.

Sunday World, 1 September 1996

THOMAS HARDY
LONELY MASTER OF PROSE AND VERSE

We are living in an age when literary scholarship has taken the form of diligent endeavours to collate an author's work with his life; admirers of Joyce need no telling.

The quest isn't always in vain: the books about Thomas Wolfe are on sound ground: almost all of his work is autobiographical – seldom had a writer less of a secret life.

You could say much the same about D. H. Lawrence: his major novels are intensely autobiographical; he left little for the literary detectives.

Thomas Hardy could hardly provide a greater contrast to Wolfe and Lawrence: he was as secretive as a pine marten and, I suspect, as lonely as a spider.

And it is doubtful if even the most diligent mole could satisfactorily relate Hardy's life to his work.

Most people – and especially writers – have a secret life that they guard as fiercely as a mother hawk minds her chicks.

This secret life has little to do with melodrama or even drama: it is made up of happenings the significance of which are known only to the person himself.

If known outside his own mind, he would be humiliated; proverbially, no man is a hero to his valet – no man is a hero to himself.

Hardy trained as an architect but practised for only a

little while; at an early age he discovered that he could make a living by the pen.

And for a great many years he was a professional writer: most of his novels were written to order; many were first published in serial form. And they bear the almost inevitable flaws of this constriction.

And yet almost all his novels have memorable passages: the poet in him couldn't be suppressed.

When eventually he became independent of the publishers, he began to write for himself.

Three of his novels came out of this matrix: *Tess of the d'Urbervilles*, *The Mayor of Casterbridge* and *Jude the Obscure*.

The Mayor of Casterbridge owes nothing to Hardy's own experience; the other two novels almost certainly do.

Tess Durbeyfield is Hardy's most convincing portrait of a woman.

The character is without doubt based on his mother: like Tess, she was a servant girl – and like Tess she was seduced, but unlike Tess she was not betrayed.

Jemima Hand was a remarkable woman. Her family background was littered with violence, alcoholism and illegitimacy, but she rose above it: she was a Mother Courage who saw to it that all of her children got a good education.

Thomas was a delicate child and was reared very close to the apron strings – his knowledge of a servant girl's life was imbibed from his mother.

The Tess we meet in the novel is very much a real person, at least for the greater part of the narrative. She is honest and diligent and has a great capacity for loving.

You feel for her – until she murders the man who has

betrayed her. This act is so entirely out of character that the remainder of the novel is incredible.

We have seen drama degenerate into melodrama. You can argue that the Victorian age abounded in melodrama, but there is a limit.

A good woman doesn't suddenly become a murderess.

Hardy attempted to wash away the incredulity by postulating that Tess was driven by forces outside herself.

The famous last sentence is often quoted: 'The President of the Immortals had finished his sport with Tess.' It is a ludicrous concept.

The Mayor of Casterbridge tells the story of Michael Henchard, the farm labourer who rose to become the head of his community.

He is an incredible figure. And if you summarised the plot, it would read like a send-up of the Victorian novel.

It is unique in one aspect: Hardy was an astonishingly independent writer – he seemed to owe nothing to anyone – but in Michael Henchard's descent to ruin there are obvious parallels with *King Lear*.

You can fault Hardy for his plots and his unreal characters but not for his writing: it is almost always fresh and bold and very much his own.

And yet there is a paradox latent within it: there are times when his boldness seems to desert him.

And he invokes classical references as if to heighten his narrative, as if unconfident of the worthiness of his local world as material for art.

You will find a similar seeming diffidence in Canon Sheehan's novels: he frequently moves from the local to the exotic as if to heighten his narrative.

Jude the Obscure was Hardy's last novel and is deemed to be his greatest.

When you have read it, you may understand why T. S. Eliot dismissed him as 'the village atheist'.

I am loath to deem it great; it is too dark; it is as if Hardy set out to take pessimism to its ultimate end.

And it evokes a principle articulated by the great critic Desmond McCarthy – that no matter how grey the world portrayed, you must have a sense of a better world outside it.

Emile Zola's greatest novel, *L'Assommoir*, is an example: it is a story of almost unremitting sadness and tragedy but its heroine could have been happy if she had better judgement.

When the world is as dark as in *Jude the Obscure*, there is no tragedy – because all life is tragic.

Jude Fawley is a country boy who aspires to be a great scholar; his life goes against him.

He is trapped into marriage by a vulgar girl, Arabella, who pretends that she is pregnant.

There is one especially memorable passage in this novel.

One morning Jude has a pig to kill – but the butcher fails to come.

Arabella taunts Jude for his lack of masculinity as the killing of the pig falls to him.

Hardy never worked as a rural labourer but he was an acute observer – the passage about the killing of the pig is unforgettable in its realism.

When you rope a pig to put a ring in his nose, he will squeal; when you rope a pig to bring him to be killed, he will utter a terrible cry from the heart.

It is a cry you will never forget; every killing of a pig is a harrowing experience.

Sue Bridehead is the heroine of *Jude the Obscure*; she is trapped in a loveless marriage to a man who desired her because she was intelligent, educated and beautiful.

She is what American sociologists – God save us from them – would call a trophy wife.

Jude the Obscure has been labelled the first feminist novel – and Sue has been described as the first modern woman in fiction.

Admirers of H. G. Wells would hardly agree – but that's another story.

Sue gets away from her legal spouse; Jude too strikes out on his own. Their paths converge; they decide to make their lives together – but they do not live happily ever after.

If Hardy's last novel reflects his vision of the world, you cannot but suspect that his own life was very bleak indeed.

His first marriage seems to have been disastrous: acres of forest have been levelled to provide paper for analysing it.

Emma was born higher up in the social scale than Hardy; she seems to have been a snob; what is certain is that she had an extremely narrow mind in the context of religion.

Hardy married again when he was in his seventies: Florence seems to have been more congenial – but there is little to hint that she brought him happiness.

The truth seems to be that Hardy loved womankind (that is palpable in his poetry) but couldn't love an individual woman – except, of course, his mother.

And it is probably true to say that writers aren't real

people at all: life to them is only material for their work.

Hardy's life bristles with paradoxes: the greatest is that this cold, mean man bequeathed us a marvellous treasure house in prose and in poetry. All of his novels, despite their flaws, are worth reading.

He was a great teller of stories: a brilliant example is his poem 'The Turnip Hoer'.

Ike one day is at his work in the fields when he hears a commotion coming from the nearby road.

Over the crest of a hill he sees a pair of horses that have bolted; a lady in an open carriage is screaming.

Ike dashes on to the road and brings the runaways to a halt. He is well rewarded – but that isn't the end of the story.

For a few moments he had held the beautiful, aristocratic lady in his arms: he is smitten.

In an especially poignant stanza, we find him indifferent to his dinner. His wife asks, 'What's wrong? Don't you like me any more?'

Ike, the diligent, thrifty labourer, spends all his savings on drink; eventually he is found dead on the railway track.

The story exemplifies Hardy's most famous dictum: 'At the graveside of even the humblest man you see his life as dramatic.'

Evening Press, 23 February 1994

Fountain of Youth
Growing Up with Water

The story of my childhood is intimately bonded with three rivers, none of which has a legal name or even a generally accepted name.

The biggest of the three has its origin in the north-east of the great saucer that geographers call the Castle Island Gap.

Even though it has no official title, it has given a name – and a lovely name – to a hill and to an electoral district: Gleannsharoon, 'the valley of the bitter apples'.

Some people call it 'the Gleannsharoon River'; others call it 'Twomey's River' because its best fishing stretch flows by land owned by a family of that name.

The bitter apples – crab apples, if you like – are in abundance in what you might call the middle stretch of the river.

You will see them in three colours: yellow, green and red.

When we were very small boys, we tried various schemes to make those apples reasonably sweet.

Our last resort was to put them into hay for a few weeks; this experiment in chemistry failed.

All, however, wasn't lost. Our mothers welcomed those rejects: they made excellent crab-apple jelly.

One part of the crab-tree section is especially interesting:

it bears a remarkable name – *rí na n-asal*, 'the king of the asses'.

Therein lies a nice little piece of social history: 'the king of the asses' was a man without land but not without resource.

Parts of the river were fenced off to prevent animals from straying: little 'inches' were left in places between the fence and the river.

The king's asses grazed in those little parcels of no man's land; I need hardly add that they never lacked for water.

A little distance downstream from this kingdom there is a strange little citadel known as Lamb's Island.

Nobody seems certain about its ownership; it is on the boundary between two farms.

The river runs by it on the eastern side; a half-circle of marsh justifies the word 'island'.

Whenever I stood on that citadel, I felt it was a non-human place, that nobody had ever tilled it or grazed it.

Folklore told us it had got its name from a man called Lamb, a criminal who hid there and came to a bad end. I suspect, however, that the truth was more prosaic.

A few hundred yards downstream from Lamb's Island, a stretch of the river is liberally adorned with black alders; here, for some reason best known to themselves, is a habitat of Europe's smallest bird, the goldcrest.

You could go through a long life without seeing one – or you might see one in the distance and mistake it for a butterfly. Often when you are bait-fishing, you are almost motionless: the magical little creature probably mistakes you for a tree and moves around freely.

When the river debouches into Old Father Maine, there

is a high chalk bank on its western side; there you can see the occasional lightning flash of the kingfisher, mesmerising in its array of colours.

Here near the junction is the legendary Gerald's Pool, a little bay dug out so that cattle can drink; fish rest in its calm during a flood.

There I caught the finest trout of my life: not the biggest, but the best-proportioned – a beautiful two-and-three-quarter-pounder.

And there a friend of mine caught the biggest fluke ever known in our neck of the waters: it weighed a little over three pounds.

These strange creatures, known elsewhere as flounders, seem ill-equipped for an aquatic life but get by. They love calm, sandy bottoms: in the Gleannsharoon River there is a fluke line above which they do not go.

That same river used to abound in brown trout: I hope it still does. You would meet the occasional white trout in it but not very often and then usually in the Spring.

It is a limestone river – and white trout, known elsewhere as sea trout, seem to prefer softer water.

Incidentally, I have long believed that white trout are brown trout that spent a while at sea – but that's a story for another day.

A few miles west from the origin of the Crab Apple River you will come to a brown stream that rises in the bog above Fahaduff.

For the first mile or so of its life it recalls Yeats's 'Pools among the rushes that scarce could bathe a star' – it keeps only little trout.

And yet that stretch is very dear to me. It ends in a

waterfall: in my childhood it seemed to me the most beautiful sight in the whole wide world.

And in later life I came to understand why Edvard Grieg was so inspired by the waterfalls of his native Norway.

Just above the waterfall there is – or used to be – a short cut which saves a few miles for the traveller from our town to Fahaduff.

Twice a woman perished there, not realising how much the water had risen since she had gone to the town.

Fish cannot go over the waterfall because its neck is too high – and yet there are fish above it.

The heron, known locally as the crane, supplies the answer: it eats and excretes spawn. Thus it resembles Johnny Appleseed, the legendary pioneer whose mission in life was to spread orchards throughout America.

About half a mile downstream from the waterfall you will come to a water junction – a cumar, as it is known locally.

There the river of the waterfall is joined by a stream that originates in the townland of Foyle, the Cliff.

It flows so rapidly that it contains few fish and those are little; that is why it is almost all covered over with bushes. We used to call it a glen and left it to the fox and the badger.

Here, at this junction or cumar, the river of the waterfall reaches a townland called Tulligabeen – and this was the name we gave to it.

Tulligabeen plays a part in our family tree; 'family bush' might be more apt.

One of my old man's grandfathers. Mike Houlihan, spent most of his life there, though hardly by choice.

He had fled thither from Caherciveen to avoid being charged for sheep-stealing; seemingly he didn't fancy the alternatives of the hangman's rope or transportation to Australia.

He managed to rent a few fields in Tulligabeen, kept an exceedingly low profile and got by.

Eventually the law caught up with him but by then they probably decided he had done his penance.

They caught up with him in the context of a murder that was still a topic around the firesides in my young manhood.

It is a strange story: it begins with a married couple who worked a substantial farm in the high country in the parish of Ballymacelligott.

Seemingly the marriage wasn't going too well. She wanted rid of him; she conspired with one of her cousins who lived in Fahaduff.

The murder was planned for a day in November; the household wasn't out of turf but the good woman hid the little that remained and despatched her husband to the mountain.

When he arrived at the rick, the cousin was waiting for him, armed with a Colt .45 that had seen service in the American Civil War.

The hitman wasted no time. He then untackled the horse; when the animal came galloping home into the yard, the good woman knew that the fell deed was done.

The killer then made all haste to establish an alibi; he sped on foot to a townland called Dooneen; it stands high on the Gleannsharoon River.

It was late November, in the proverbial 'idle times'; a

dance was being held in a farmhouse there.

Nobody doubted the identity of the killer. When the news of the murder became known next day, it had a terrible effect on a girl with whom he danced; ever after, she was obsessed with washing her hands.

The killer was arrested and duly tried. Among the principal witnesses were some men who had been working on the road not far from the rick. It had been a very misty day: they had seen nothing but they had heard the fatal shots.

Now Mike Houlihan enters the story: he had been digging spuds when the hitman passed through the field, taking, so he said, a short cut to Dooneen – incidentally, by way of the waterfall.

My great-grandfather gave false testimony: he swore his neighbour had passed through the field earlier than he actually had.

The RIC brought one of their members, a famous long-distance runner, to travel the eight-odd miles. He couldn't match the time – it was little wonder.

The hitman went free.

The third river that threaded its way through my childhood is a modest stream that comes down from a townland called Curranes. I loved it because it was so peaceful; it is in a deep valley; you could be in another world.

And where it joins the Tulligabeen River, they make a lovely cumar. It is calm water and yet wonderfully alive, a most fertile place in a flood.

The Tulligabeen River abounded in brown trout. When first I fished along its stream, I was about nine – and the more I went downstream, the more fruitful it became.

Alas, about two miles from where it enters Old Man Maine, it diminishes as some of the water goes underground; this discovery was one of the great disappointments of my young life.

Flow on, lovely rivers.

Evening Press, 6 April 1994

The Hare
Creature of Myth and Magic

The definition of 'hare' in the *Chambers Modern English Dictionary* will amuse those who are acquainted with that remarkable creature: 'a common and very timid and very swift mammal'. The hare may look timid but the male will fight – though not quite to the death – with his rivals at mating time and will swim surprising distances across rough seas obeying the same instinct.

For good measure, this shy but untimid creature has played a fair part in language and mythology.

People can be described as hare-brained; we can run with the hound and the hare; we can let the hare sit.

And it occurs in a smattering of place names.

Knocknagree, a famous village on the border of Cork and Kerry, seems to be an example.

If you happen to have grown up in the country, you are likely to have heard strange tales about the hare.

Stealing milk from your neighbours' cows seems to have been a popular form of private enterprise in not-so-ancient Ireland: the hare played its part.

I hasten to add that when a cow was found yielding less than her expected share at the morning milking, the culprit was usually the hedgehog – and it didn't bring a bottle.

Peasants are, however, a suspicious breed: it was better to blame some neighbour with whom you weren't on good terms.

The woman of the family was always the culprit: she carried out her fell deeds in the form of the hare.

And inevitably you will be told about the man who got tired of having his milk stolen – and decided to take desperate measures.

At last one dawn his vigil was rewarded. He spotted a hare among his herd; he fired a shot; the hare fled – but left a trail of blood.

It led to a neighbour's cottage; there he found that the woman of the house was being treated for gunshot wounds.

This, I suspect, is an international folk tale, but I have often heard it retailed with an abundance of local colour.

And in my young days I was solemnly assured by my elders that a hare was capable of doing a vanishing act.

Sometimes when hotly pursued, it might take refuge in a ringfort – a fairy fort, as it was sometimes known in rural idiom – then it would disappear.

And of course down in the south-west of Ireland we had our own version of the rope trick: we wouldn't let it go with the Indians.

I love the little story about a rather strange happening that took place in our town.

It was a market day: down by the Fountain, which is more or less the focus of the town, a little man whom nobody had ever seen before put two bags down on the ground and began to make a speech.

And he unfolded a strange promise. He produced a rope from one bag and a hare from the other. The rope would go up into the sky – and the hare would use it to ascend out of sight.

And so seemingly it came to pass. The strange man duly

collected mites of silver and copper. One member of the gathering was not impressed: he had seen nothing but a man with his right hand outstretched.

He was a poor man who happened to be passing by with a sack of fresh grass for his cow.

When he emptied the sack, he found that it had contained a four-leaf clover. Now he understood why he hadn't seen the rope and the hare: the four-leaf clover is a safeguard against magic. Now there's a piece of extremely useful information for you.

All these folk beliefs may originate in fantasy. There is, however, one aspect of the hare's life that is akin to magic: 'How does the species survive?'

The hare is almost unique among our wild animals in that it isn't equipped to defend itself from its natural enemies, nor has it a counterpart of the rabbit's burrow and the fox's den and the badger's set.

The hare sleeps in the open. His 'form' may be in a clump of grass or rushes or heather. Sometimes he may lie in ploughland or even in a little hollow in a bare field.

His great peripheral vision and acute hearing are a help; so are his swiftness and stamina.

A bigger question remains: 'How do the young hares – the leverets – survive?' You will see no more beautiful creatures. They are born with all their fur and with perfect sight; this does not preclude them from looking hopelessly vulnerable.

One factor helps them survive: the mother doesn't put all her young in one basket; she hides them individually. The usual number in a litter is three – and they may be hidden in an area of a few acres.

There may be a second factor: those country people who love the hare will tell you that the leveret is entirely without scent.

When I first heard this, I found it incredible. I am not so sure now. How else do you explain why so many leverets survive the predation of the stoat and the fox?

There is another folk belief which may contain a grain of truth: some of my neighbours would tell you that there is an Irish hare as distinct from the hare familiar to most of us.

The Irish hare is small and dark-brown, almost black. This belief fits in with the notion that the indigenous Irish cow is small and black and that the indigenous Irish hen is also small and black.

And of course there is Cúchulainn. He too was small and black, and he was here before Fionn and the Fianna – they were only blow-ins.

I spent a great deal of time engaged in what is known as country coursing but only twice did I meet a hare that was small and almost black. I will tell you more about that in due course.

I might as well tell you what country coursing is. It is akin to what is known as open coursing, only more casually organised.

Men of like mind come together on Sunday mornings in the season or on some other free day and set out for the fields or the hills or the mountains.

The aficionados of country coursing have a very strict ethic. Newcomers are taught the rules, and woe betide him who steps out of line.

When you 'rise' a hare ('put up' is the term in the other

island), the nearest two hounds are slipped – but only after the hare has been given a fair 'lead'.

The aficionados of country coursing revere the hare and abhor a kill, if only for pragmatic reasons.

The sport has long since developed a lore and a language of its own.

There is, for instance, a strong and well-founded belief that if a hare gets up on three feet, it is exceptional and is most unlikely to be caught.

There is also the 'game hare': this is another exceptional example of the species.

It frequents the same small area of ground and seems to delight in leading the hounds the proverbial merry dance.

I knew an exceptional example of this exceptional breed: she (we eventually discovered her gender) was invariably 'risen' or 'put up' in a little area of bog at the bottom of a fertile farm.

She was far bigger than the average and in one great bound always flew free: no hound could get near her.

Alas, hares are very vulnerable in heavy snow: this particular one was captured by a collie in the terrible February of 1947.

Every inland hare has what is called a 'run'; a mountain hare doesn't need one, as you will see.

The run is an escape route. It is of course predetermined – and the hare will do all it can to stay on that survival causeway.

It may turn ninety degrees or more but will strive with all its agility and cunning to get back to the main route.

And eventually the final act of escape comes when the hare goes under a gate or through a hole in a fence or even runs through a gullet or culvert.

Sometimes when a hare is under fierce pressure, it may escape by a simple and brilliant ploy. It may come to a bush or a bunch of rushes in the middle of a field and turn at a hundred and eighty degrees; the dogs go flying past. Their momentum carries them far beyond the bush or the bunch of rushes; this ploy is known as 'blinking the hounds'.

Occasionally you will get a hound, usually a bitch, that makes no attempt to catch the hare: it will curve around the side and hope that the other hound will drive the hare into its path.

This is known as 'poaching'. It can put the hare off its run – and exceptional speed and cunning will be needed for survival.

The most remarkable course I ever saw seems unreal in the memory, almost a fantasy.

On a Sunday long ago we rose a hare in a big field on a farm that slopes down from the Dublin road near a summit well known to travellers: Gleannsharoon. The two men nearest the hare were inexperienced – and for a few moments we thought, to our horror, that they had slipped at a leveret.

Little did we know: this little dark-brown hare was straight out of mythology: a super specimen of its tribe.

It wasn't especially swift but its elusiveness was mesmerising: time and again it eluded what appeared certain capture.

Eventually it made its way to the field next to the road; now the hounds were labouring.

And when they got close to the little magician, it didn't turn: it merely shifted a little to either side.

The hounds were not now turning the hare: they were 'wrenching' it.

The course lasted about three minutes before the little hero or heroine ran through the farmyard and across the Dublin road.

We never encountered that small dark-brown hare again.

How could we justify our coursing? You will hear spurious reasons.

The truth is that we were obsessed with this almost-mystical creature – and we were thrilled by the sight of two hounds in pursuit of it.

Some people call it 'the dance of death'. Sometimes it is; more often it is the dance of life.

I have rarely seen a hare fail to escape on the mountain. There they need no 'run': when they escape the first five or six turns, their stamina will do the rest.

The hare is not unknown in art and literature.

One of Dürer's most famous paintings is a portrait of a hare.

You will find charming passages in William Cowper's diaries about his pet hares.

And of course there is Oliver Goldsmith's simile about his wish to return home to Ireland:

> And as a hare whom hounds and horns pursue
> Pants to the place from which at first she flew.

We will let William Wordsworth have the last say:

> All things that love the sun are out of doors;
> The sky rejoices in the morning's birth;
> The grass is bright with raindrops; on the moors
> The Hare is running races in her mirth.

And with her feet she from the plashy earth
Raises a mist that glittering in the sun
Runs with her all the way, wherever she doth run.

Evening Press, 19 October 1994

Liam Brady
Two-footed Perfectionist

I remember it well, even though a lot of wine and beer and spirits has gone down the red lane in the meantime.

It was in October of 1974 and I was then scraping a living doing bits and pieces for Radio Éireann and the *Irish Press*.

Nevertheless, I was looking forward in high excitement to the imminent clash of the Republic and the Soviets in Dalymount Park.

And to soothe my seething mind I adjourned to the Harp, that seductive oasis near O'Connell Bridge.

There I was joined by a colleague, Sean Ward, then in his formative years as editor of the *Evening Press*.

Another colleague who had better be nameless had told us that there was very little interest in the match even though it was in the qualifying round for the World Cup.

That colleague specialised in Soccer – and so we took his word as gospel.

And we were in no great hurry to go to the North Circular Road.

And we had an abundance to talk about on that Wednesday afternoon long ago.

Muhammad Ali had just unmanned George Foreman away down below in Zaire.

And a great little man called Joe who sported a turned-down pipe and a vibrant typewriter had departed this mortal life below in Rhodesia.

I can still recall the headline in the *Evening Press*: 'All Is Quiet Now in Sherwood Forest'.

That act of memory is no great feat; after all, I wrote it myself.

Anyway, Sean and myself didn't leave the Harp until a quarter of an hour before the time for the tip-off; little did we know.

There wasn't a taxi to be had in the centre of Dublin; panic set in.

Resourceful as ever, I hijacked a van driven by an old friend, John Heaney, who was then working for Max Florist.

And he whisked us up to the old grey stadium that was then the venue for all our home internationals.

An amazing scene awaited us: the gates were locked – the ground was full for over half an hour.

We went around to the Tramway end: there some enterprising citizens were working like their counterparts in 1789 who stormed the Bastille.

Eventually the gates gave way. Hundreds flooded in: it was a bizarre prelude to the first occasion on which I watched Liam Brady play.

And in this context 'play' in the appropriate word: the lad from Whitehall looked as carefree as if playing on a beach.

The Soviet midfielders didn't look so happy; indeed, they resembled hens that had suddenly found a cub in their midst.

John Keats wished that his first book of poems would explode upon the world: it didn't get as much as a single review.

I doubt if Liam Brady harboured any such ambition, but

on that grey, windy afternoon long ago, he most certainly exploded onto the Football world.

And he helped my neighbour Don Givens to write the greatest chapter in his Football story.

Don did the hat-trick – and an astounded world heard that the Republic had beaten the USSR 3–0.

At the time, I had never met Liam – and for years afterwards I knew him only by a few remarks exchanged across crowded rooms.

I knew that his mother used to send him bits and pieces that I had written about him: it was a link of a kind.

And then one morning in Malta the phone rang in my hotel room – as phones tend to do – and the bold Liam was at the other end.

And we adjourned to a quiet corner of a very quiet bar in the ancient city of San Antonio, which is surely the quietest place in the whole wide world.

It was on the day after that crazy game in the Ta'Qali Stadium when a black wind blew up from Africa and the Republic won by Frank Stapleton's late late goal.

That morning Liam and I had a conversation so frank and intimate that in retrospect it seems unreal.

As a people the Irish remind me of what Arnold Bennett said about his neighbours in the Potteries: 'Full of crushed tenderness.'

We are very reluctant to express our deeper feelings, lest we be thought soft.

Sometimes for some reason very difficult to divine, we suspend our reticence.

And that morning on the stony little island called Malta there was a rare outpouring.

I suppose part of the cause was that we had much in common.

We both came from the working class before it was popular or profitable to do so.

And we both worked at rather strange trades: basically, professional footballers and professional writers are entertainers.

And, if I may say so, we both suffer from an incurable ailment called perfectionism.

Anyhow, that morning we spoke about our hopes and ambitions and about lovely ships that had passed in the night.

And I discovered something that I had long suspected: Liam Brady is a highly intelligent and deeply sensitive man.

He is also a very generous one: on the evening on which we came back from Iceland in September of 1983, he bought a round of drinks for about thirty of us in the bar at Dublin Airport.

Some people might say that he could well afford it, but that isn't the point – it was a nice gesture.

There is little need for me to evaluate Liam as a footballer: his record shouts for itself.

Most of his admirers will tell you that his greatest-ever display was for Arsenal in that famous Cup final with Manchester United.

They have a strong case but I would be inclined to nominate another occasion.

It was a dark, windy Saturday afternoon at Highbury. It was a league match; Everton were the visitors.

I stood with the Kop on the South Bank. We enjoyed a fine game; it ended in a draw.

Liam played superbly – and for good measure scored a remarkable goal.

He made a little run down the inside-left channel; he seemed about to be closed out on the verge of the box. He let fly with his right foot – and scored.

Until that moment, everybody in Football was convinced that his right was merely there for balancing.

I can still see the look of astonishment on his marker's face. Was it Colin Todd?

I last met Liam – for more than a few minutes, that is – on the morning after the Republic had beaten England in the European Cup.

It was a little after dawn and I was walking in the Black Forest, high above Stuttgart.

So was Liam. I cannot remember what we spoke about; all I know is that we didn't mention Football.

Liam couldn't but have been a little sad – but he could console himself that he played a mighty part in getting our team to West Germany.

The good peasant plants and tends the vine even though he may not be around to drink the wine.

from the programme for Liam Brady's testimonial

Dublin Marathon
Flow on Lovely River

It happened for the seventeenth time on Monday. The Dublin Marathon took me back to my childhood. It was about seven o'clock on a May morning; my brother and myself were waiting at the gate of our cottage for Duffy's Circus on its way from Abbeyfeale to Castle Island.

We were inside the gate because we had been warned not to go outside it lest we be eaten up by elephants. We knew that they were coming on foot – if foot is the right word.

After about half an hour that seemed like a sample of eternity, their great grey bulks came into view at the turn about three hundred yards up the road. There were two of them; two men on horseback were close behind.

The elephants were obedient but not subservient; now and then they stopped to eat clumps out of thorn hedges. They did even better: across the road from our house there was a pyramid of fragmented stones that the county council had for repairing the road – alas . . .

The elephants dipped their great trunks deep into the pile and blew the fragments high into the air and all over the place. We were delighted.

Even though I was only about six at the time, I was surprised that they were so much at home several thousand miles from the land of their ancestors. You could say that they were laid back, if that term had been going around at the time.

By the time I was about seven, I had decided to make my living as an angler, and this vocation involved another kind of waiting.

In the great saucer-valley of which Castle Island is the centre, it happens sometimes that the rain falls on some of the hills but not on the lowlands; therein lies a tale.

Whenever I saw it raining heavily up near a hill called Crinna, I knew that soon there would be a flood on our beloved Gleannsharoon River and I used to go down to my favourite spot and wait.

That hill was about five miles away and sometimes I might be waiting for perhaps an hour; then you perceived a faint colouring of the water – that was the first sign.

Then the familiar harbingers used to come: leaves and pieces of driftwood and maybe even twigs. The flood was on its way.

I remember other waitings, especially for the multistage cycle races. The first came in the year of that crazy festival called 'An Tostal'.

I can still see Shay Elliott in the yellow jersey as he led the field up the hill past our house on the way from Killarney to Limerick. Thenceforth, I followed his career as closely as if he had been my brother.

On Monday there was a fair scattering of people outside the Oval bar. At about ten past eleven the grapevine told us that the leaders were in Parkgate Street. In fact, they were nearer.

Soon came the gardai in their clearly marked car; then came the good people of Seiko with their marvellous digital clock on bright-yellow alert.

Then you could hear the spattering of applause increase – and soon the leader came into view, a quintessential Kenyan, ebony and long-limbed and sculpted for long-distance running.

I doubt if anyone in the little crowd in front of the Oval knew his name but he was warmly applauded and responded with a great flash of teeth. He was running as if he knew he had won, and so he had – his two other countrymen were a minute behind.

They too got their mead of applause. The next runner got an ovation: Tommy Maher, a staunch son of Meath, is familiar to watchers of the Dublin Marathon. He was fifth last year in 2:23 – on Monday he finished in 2:21.

About twenty to twelve, the leading woman sailed in. Catherine Shum was all flowing yellow hair and smiles. She is a native of Santry but lives in Burton-on-Trent.

I couldn't but wonder at the grace and power of the Kenyans: Joseph Kahuba, Mbarack Hussein, Joshua Kipkemboi and John Kipyato. I suspect that in a previous incarnation they were mountain hares.

Though thousands of miles from Mount Kenya on a grey, windy Dublin day, they seemed as perfectly at home as the two elephants on that May morning long ago.

Long-distance runners do not like the wind. I saw it at its wildest about half past ten in Cuffe Street: there the sodden leaves were whirling in a crazy dance.

Most of the runners were crouching with heads bent, but in the middle of the road a wee lad of about seven was running very erect and with head back: he was running a marathon in his dreams.

When the first twenty or so of the runners had passed

the Oval, I went down along the quay. The best way to recognise people is when they are coming towards you: several friends waved to me.

In almost all the previous Dublin Marathons, you could expect the pack about two and a half hours after the start, but this year it wasn't so. The leaves and the pieces of driftwood and the twigs came but not the flood.

It was about ten past twelve when something resembling a pack came and even this was unusually strung out – the wind seemed to have taken its toll.

By one o'clock, four hours after the start, a cold rain was blowing along the river. Most of the watchers went away – and the late runners had only the gardai at the junctions to encourage them. They surely experienced the loneliness of the long-distance runner.

This year there was no big Kerry interest. Jerry Kiernan and John Griffin have retired. I transferred my allegiance to Seamus Cawley – he is from Rathkeale.

Seamus is a quiet hero. He has competed in all seventeen Dublin Marathons and completed them all in under three hours. On Monday he came home in 2:59.

By about half past one I had got a fair drenching for the second time in two days and I retired to the Boar's Head in Capel Street, a little pub that my dear departed friend Tom Hourican made great.

His kinsman, Hughie, is now on the bridge and is carrying on the good work. There on Monday I encountered a fair galaxy of nurses from James's and Saint Patrick's and got enough hugs to do me until the Golden Pages go walkabout again.

Sunday World, 3 November 1996

IRELAND'S TRAVELLING MINSTRELS
FIDDLERS ON THE HOOF

The concept of the generation gap was produced by some American sociologist on a day when he had nothing better to do.

There were about thirty-five years between Patrick Keeffe the great fiddle player, and me, but we couldn't have been closer friends: we spoke the same language.

Patrick was born in Glounthane, a townland about five miles to the east of Castle Island. One night long ago on the radio, I heard Ciaran MacMathuna ask Patrick where is Glounthane. The answer was pithy: 'Glounthane is where the bog is.'

Indeed it is – and for good measure it is in the very heart of Sliabh Luachra, a region that in recent years has become a moveable feast and is now threatening to embrace all Munster.

Patrick trained as a teacher in Drumcondra, and while there he won the gold medal at the All-Ireland Feis. Incidentally, he set little store by this achievement – and indeed he disliked competitions.

One day when he was the adjudicator at Ballyheigue Fleadh, he chose a quiet corner on the stage and fell gently asleep. When asked to give his judgement, he said, 'They were all good.'

Patrick began his working life as a teacher in Glounthane

National School, where his parents had taught before him.

He was a good teacher but the profession was not for him: he was a free-range spirit.

'Connie boy, whenever there was a fair in Castle Island or a race meeting in Knocknagree or maybe a neighbour getting married, the four walls of the school were like the confines of a prison.'

There were days when he didn't turn up. His absences became more frequent and more prolonged. It was all too bad to last.

And one morning when he came to the school, he found a young man sitting at his table; a rather taut silence ensued.

High noon approached. In this context it was half past nine, the official time for calling the roll; the young man opened the ledger.

Patrick got up and went towards the door. The young man spoke to him for the first time: 'Take that thing with you.'

'That thing' was his beloved fiddle; those two words in themselves tell you what little appreciation there was for country music in that barren era.

Patrick was then little over thirty. There was no social welfare in those days; he was to survive without any kind of regular income. It was a daunting prospect.

He made a living of a kind by teaching the fiddle. As they say in Kerry, he saw more dinner times than dinners.

He was never a man to complain. He had made his own bed – and sometimes it was a bed of nails.

There is a wealth of stories about him. Some are true; some have long ago passed into common lore and are told about other folk figures.

My favourite is known to almost everyone on this island: 'I went to Scartaglen last Sunday night and left the bike against the wall outside O'Connor's pub. When I came out, the wall was there but the bike was gone.'

One night he failed to turn up for a recording session organised by Ciaran MacMathuna in Castle Island. Now read on . . .

It was little wonder: the mountain country was under snow. Patrick's little house stood where two roads intersect – and therein hangs the tale.

When Ciaran met him a few weeks later, he asked Patrick why he didn't turn up. 'Like Jesus Christ was nailed to the cross in Calvary, I was nailed to the cross in Glounthane,' Patrick replied.

Humour was the great anodyne in those days when penury stalked the land. The fiddle players were very adept at it.

Denis Murphy, another marvellous musician, was very quick on the verbal draw.

He took up a job in New York and eventually he was joined by Jerry McCarthy, another virtuoso on the fiddle.

On Jerry's first night in the Big Apple, my friend Denis took him to his favourite pub in the Bronx.

They weren't too long there when the sound of gunfire came from the street, and Jerry said: 'What are they firing at?' And Denis said: 'I'll tell you one thing for sure – it isn't a fox.'

They both worked as porters in the Metropolitan Gallery at the time when the *Mona Lisa* was on loan and thousands of schoolchildren were being brought from all over the US to view it.

Jerry, God rest him, had a remarkable face – the kind you see in El Greco paintings. It was long and pale and bony and crowned with a cluster of black curls and illuminated by great brown eyes. Therein hangs a tale: when Denis was home on holiday, he said to me, 'Connie, they weren't coming to see the *Mona Lisa;* they were coming to see McCarthy.'

Jerry himself was no slouch at catching in the wry – and I recall with a mixture of fondness and sadness a little paragraph from our lives and hard times.

It belongs to an era when I was the headmaster in the Church of Ireland school in Ballymacelligott. It wasn't a position of great honour: it was a one-teacher school.

Jerry was teaching the fiddle to one of the rector's sons. One evening the two of us set out on foot for home together. The roads were frost-bound; there were no buses.

About halfway on our journey, we were assailed by nibs of snow and pellets of hail. We took shelter under a hawthorn bush that had seen better days.

And Jerry said: 'Do you know something, Coneen – we're like Napoleon's army on the retreat from Moscow.'

Patrick Keeffe had the reputation of being fond of the drink but I never saw him the worse for it.

Bill Shankly, the great Football manager, would have understood – even though he was a teetotaller.

He grew up in a mining town in Lanarkshire and in his autobiography he wrote: 'Almost all my neighbours drank a lot. You couldn't blame them. They did very hard work for very low pay. They drank to keep themselves from going mad.'

You couldn't say that Patrick O'Keeffe died from drink:

he was well into his seventies when he passed away.

And there was a certain irony in his passing: he died not from drink but for the lack of it.

It was a bitter Winter. For a week in January, his little house was snow-bound. He couldn't go to Castle Island or Scartaglen for his nightly intake.

He got pneumonia and was taken to hospital in Tralee; there he died about three o'clock on a Friday.

His neighbour, Kate Mannix, was on the way up the stairs, accompanied by a bottle of Paddy, when a nurse told her that her old friend had just died.

I got on the phone to RTÉ – and, fair dues to them, they gave him a good show on the News at Six. Nobody deserved it better.

XPress, 17 July 1995

Irishmen on Tour

I know who invented the steam engine, the aeroplane, the safety pin, the washing board, the non-stick frying pan, the combustion engine and the modern *sliotar* – but not, strangely enough, who invented the bicycle.

It is a woefully deep flaw in my armour. The bicycle in its own quiet and humble way has changed the world so much that you could legitimately talk of the pre-bicycle age and the bicycle age.

And you could also borrow a few words from poetry and refer to the bicycle as a thing of beauty and a joy forever.

A generation ago, or perhaps two, in this country you could hear grown men and ungrown men arguing furiously about the virtues of various makes, so much so that a visitor who didn't know the language might have thought that they were arguing about their horses.

In my youthful fantasies I believed that you could judge a man by his bike.

The solid citizen – let him be a big farmer or a publican or a merchant – favoured the Rudge; the common man preferred the Raleigh; the yuppie – as yet unchristened – went for the BSA or the Royal Enfield.

And of course the super-yuppie went in for the low-slung handlebars; he mightn't be a racing cyclist but at least he could look like one.

And of course the gearcase was a powerful symbol; it

was the mark of the conservative, the man who carries a raincoat even when the forecast is for dry weather and who would never forget his bicycle clips.

In those distant days we had heard about the Tour de France but it seemed to belong to a world that we would never inhabit.

Then came the first of the stage races – and great was the excitement along the route.

It was as if the outside world had come to us; we were getting a taste of the Continent.

Men from far off the main roads – men who normally you would see only on Sundays or fair days or at Duffy's Circus – came from their fastnesses to wait and watch.

People used to take up their positions long before the expected time; rumours inevitably came along, some of them more or less true; then would come the first signs that the cavalcade was imminent.

First came the outriders on motorbikes; then came the official cars; then after a little interval that seemed a sample of eternity, the leading riders appeared; soon came the bunch – we have a different name for it now.

And then the flood began to fall until a stream of stragglers came by – and inevitably a few came when only the most dedicated remained to see.

I well remember the first CRE race; the Killarney–Limerick stage went by our house; I can still clearly see Shay Elliott wearing the yellow jersey and well ahead of the pack as he powered up the four-mile hill that peaks a little beyond Gleannsharoon.

Shay was to become our great pioneer on the Continent; he would never win the Tour but did well enough in it to prove that the Continentals were not a different species.

Sean Kelly prospered on that knowledge; Stephen Roche reaped the harvest sown by Shay Elliott.

The experts tell me that Kelly is a member of a long tradition; the typical tour cyclist is a country boy, one who take hours of hard toil for granted.

Seemingly that was the pattern on the Continent until recent years; Stephen Roche is perhaps one of a new breed.

It was good to see him back this week, working quietly towards rehabilitation.

And it was good to see the infant Nissan Classic growing up so sturdily.

O'Connell Street was the capital of the cycling world for about an hour yesterday afternoon.

By four a mass of humanity crowded against the barriers even though it was well known that the race was behind schedule.

Multicoloured cars bristling with advertisements lined the quays.

The O'Connell Monument was festooned with small boys.

An exceedingly agile youth had shinned up a light standard on the bridge – I suppose you could call it the pole position.

The tannoy kept the crowd well informed; it was clear that the Irish riders wouldn't win the over-all – but that didn't seem to take from the excitement.

The harbingers were the same as ever; I might have been back on a hillside in Kerry a generation ago, only that the motorbikes were a different breed.

Then came the company cars; the word 'Nissan' proliferated.

I was watching the toll bridge away on the horizon; there the passing cars seemed like toys.

I would like to say that I discerned the first bunch of riders as they passed it – but I didn't.

And when they came along Eden Quay, they were so close together and travelling at such a clip that I couldn't pick out one that I could name – they might as well have been starlings.

When the first flurry of excitement had passed, I went down to the traffic island near the junction of the quay and Butt Bridge.

And I was near enough to see the expressions – and once again my heart went out to those great and brave men.

In Mulligan's famous back room I watched most of the round-the-city-centre finish.

The camera, we are told, doesn't lie – but in the soft light of Autumn our capital city looked almost Continental.

And I rode in my imagination those last few miles with Phil Anderson; because he was so bold, I didn't wish to see him caught.

With his big-boned, unshaven face and his dark hair streaming behind him, he was one of the few that you could easily recognise.

At the line, he couldn't have got a greater reception if he had been one of our own.

I went up to the GPO to see some of the folk heroes in the flesh.

I spotted Charlie Mottet but hardly in the flesh, more in the skin and bone.

This little man from the Alps is more like a jockey than

a racing cyclist – but then of course they are jockeys in their own way.

Eric Vanderarden looks a member of a different species; the overall winner is a blonde, powerful Belgian; his winning of four stages in a row was a mighty feat.

I met a men in the Fagor colours – and I asked him if he had been in the race.

'Only,' he said, 'as a mechanic.' And I said to myself: 'Why the "only"?'

Do you remember the brothers Orville and Wilbur Wright who lived long ago in Dayton, Ohio? They were bicycle mechanics – in their spare time they invented the aeroplane.

Samuel Beckett
A Bleak Visionary Clad in Purple

One afternoon about ten years ago in a Dublin theatre, I attended a small play by Samuel Beckett. Two young women came in a few minutes from its conclusion – and at the end applauded in a manner which bordered on the hysterical.

Their action – you could hardly call it a reaction – symbolised, if in a rather exaggerated form, the adulation that then lapped around the alleged master.

Nothing is more seductive than fashion – and in those days you murmured the slightest word of criticism at your peril. Beckett was as compassionate as Christ, as articulate as Shakespeare – if in a rather different way – and as consummate a technician as Beethoven.

A few weeks ago, Beckett passed into eternal silence. Most of the obituaries took idolatry and pretentiousness to undreamt-of shores.

And so it is under a burden of guilt that I attempt to write about him – plus an awareness of the loneliness experienced by a little boy who wasn't altogether convinced that the emperor was clad in a shining new suit.

For a start, it might be salutary to take a cool look at some explanations of Beckett's vision – real or feigned – of life.

We have been told that it owes much to Europe's trauma

between 1939 and 1945. And perhaps it does – but Walt Whitman and Patrick MacGill, among others, experienced war at its bloodiest and emerged with their romantic vision undimmed.

And it has been said too that no one could write poetry after Auschwitz. This is a silly and portentous statement if ever there was one, if only because it implies that there is an essential difference between it and prose.

Beckett's vision – if such it can be called – is rooted in a trend that goes back at least as far as Jean Jacques Rousseau: you could, without being deemed pretentious, call his *Confessions* the literary equivalent of the Bastille's fall.

We see its hero as afflicted with weaknesses which hitherto were not deemed within the scope of literature: he is a Hamlet, but with warts and all.

You can, if you so wish, call this realism: the trend – if such it was – is illustrated by Emile Zola and to a lesser extent by Gustave Flaubert.

And certainly it surfaced in French painting of the late nineteenth century. Vincent Van Gogh, especially, spares us nothing in his depiction of the poor and the downtrodden and the mentally ill.

Painting, however, no matter how lowly the life it expresses, can hardly avoid giving it a certain air of dignity, even of heroism. Writing is almost unequalled in its power of depicting the mean and the sordid and the undignified – life's proverbial dirty underbelly.

James Joyce and T. S. Eliot took the trend into bleaker territory. Beckett seems to have set himself the task of plumbing the ultimate depths: to show us life at its most hopeless – indeed, to show us a world where hope is redundant.

Molloy in the novel that bears his name is typical of Beckett's heroes: 'lonely and afraid in a world he never made'.

He is not so old as to be close to physical immobility but he is preparing for that state. His anodyne for old age – if he ever believed in anodynes – is the power to maltreat people worse off than himself.

Krapp – he of the *Last Tape* – is perhaps better known: the short play has been performed many times.

Krapp – the name indicates Beckett's liking for juvenile puns – is a writer: at least he has the consolation that he can articulate his misery and his frustration and his hopelessness.

He might evoke the dictum 'Life being what it is, I dream of revenge' but it is rather late for contemplating anything so positive.

Beckett in the popular image is the strong, almost silent man who chisels away at language until only the essential remains.

His avoidance of public appearances enhances the image. Silence is a great mask: it hints at infinite wisdom.

Most of us have known strong, silent men who, when loosened up by a few drinks, prove to be every whit as fallible as ourselves.

Beckett's work is, of course, a mansend for academics and for the intellectual elite.

For the former, it provides an infinity of thesis-fodder; for the latter, it serves as a bludgeon with which to clobber their supposed inferiors.

The academics dote on the arcane: it keeps them – well, some of them – in their jobs. And they can go on forever explaining passages in Joyce or Beckett – and it doesn't matter if the mystery hinges on a misprint or two, or even three.

Beckett, I suspect, chanced on a mine and went on and on exploiting it. I must admit, however, that I have yet to meet an actor or actress who didn't admire his plays.

And I believe that the reason is obvious: his work for the stage is at once the quintessence of drama and the antithesis of theatre.

Actors admire him because he gave directors the minimum of scope for acting the puppeteer.

You cannot do much with a player imprisoned in a barrel or up to the neck in sand.

Waiting for Godot is the most theatrical of his plays, and it was hardly surprising that in his late years he more or less disowned it – shades of Patrick Kavanagh.

Technically, it is a mess: it lacks the clean line of *Krapp's Last Tape* and some of those pieces that we heard on radio long ago when his fame was just peeping over the horizon.

A little while ago I invoked the fable of the emperor's new suit: the comparison was, of course, an outrageous exaggeration.

It belongs to the world where you advance the non-existent so as to work on the existent: the non-viscous fluid in physics and the square root of minus one in mathematics are examples.

Of course Beckett has great virtues: his passion for language is a beacon for every writer, no matter how modest his aim.

And such people as Molloy and Krapp are as real as

Margaret Thatcher or Alex Ferguson or Pamella Bordes.

My complaint is that, real though they are, they do not exist in the real world. There is no light at the end of the tunnel or at the start of the tunnel: all is tunnel.

Desmond McCarthy, a great but now-forgotten guru of the early century, used to argue that no matter how miserable the life or lives portrayed, there should be an awareness of a better world.

It may sound a glib and even a vulgar dictum, but in a moment of confusion and bewilderment and intellectual unease I tend to come back to it.

And I cannot help feeling that two of the most acclaimed writers in post-war Europe were dishonest, if unconsciously so.

The Outsider, Albert Camus's best-known novel, was written to a formula: it came from the heyday of existentialism. So did Jean-Paul Sartre's *Nausea*. Both novels portray a world which has been channelled into a mould of the 'author's' making.

Nothing is as unfashionable as what was fashionable yesterday; I believe that both novels will in time be seen as curiosities.

And I cannot help suspecting that Samuel Beckett too wrote to a formula. For all the fineness of his intelligence, he seems to have had a closed mind.

Will much of his work too be seen as a curiosity? I don't know. Perhaps future generations will see values in it that some of this generation cannot.

I first read his novels a long time ago; some time I hope to return to them – from a sense of duty rather than in the hope of pleasure.

And should I find myself wrong, I will be delighted.

In this context, I must confess that a few days ago I had a chastening experience.

It was caused by a reader who wishes to be known as Brendan Joseph and who runs his godly race in Dublin 8: he sent me a copy of *In the Footsteps of the Master*.

Now as far as I am concerned, H. V. Morton was old hat – or perhaps merely old cap.

I had read all of his work and remembered him as a remarkable journalist but a non-starter as a 'serious' writer. How wrong can you be? The first paragraph of *In the Footsteps of the Master* brought me to my senses: 'As the sun goes down, a stillness falls over Egypt. Water channels that cross the fields turn to the colour of blood, then to bright yellow that fades into silver. The palm trees might be cut from black paper and pasted against the incandescence of the sky. Brown hawks that hang all day above the sugar cane and the growing wheat are seen no more, and one by one, the stars burn over the sandhills and lie caught in the stiff fronds of the date palms.'

You may say that this is a purple passage, but take the purple passages out of William Shakespeare's work and you wouldn't have much left.

In the Footsteps of the Master is a fine book, especially in its evocation of the desert.

It enthralled Morton, just as it enthralled Camus: the latter's great short story 'The Adulterous Woman' has nothing to do with sex and a great deal to do with sand.

Let us return to Samuel Beckett: if he never wrote a word, I would love him for the part he played in the Resistance.

And yet I must add that he perplexes me. I have heard people rave about a certain poem which he wrote late in life; I can see nothing in it.

It begins:

Folly –
Folly for to –
What is the word –
Folly from this –
All this –
Given –
Folly given all this –
Seeing –
Folly seeing all this –

And as far as I can see, it doesn't improve as it goes along.

Beckett, incidentally, was a fine Rugby player. I would like to have him in Dublin this week – and ask him to bring me fifteen hundred words on Saturday's big match at Lansdowne Road.

And I was disappointed that he didn't achieve the ultimate in drama, a play about thirty minutes in duration on a bare stage and with no players.

Of course, it would provoke a standing ovation.

Evening Press, 30 January 1990

Sliabh Luachra
A Very Movable Feast

A dozen cities boast of famous Homer dead,
Through which the living Homer begged his bread.

If in a rather different context, you could say much the same about Sliabh Luachra.

I know of no other region in Ireland that has been as romanticised in this generation.

And a question arises: 'Is it a region at all?'

It isn't a barony or a parish; it may be a townland, but I doubt it.

The sticklers for accuracy who will always be with us tell you that Sliabh Luachra is merely the name of a rushy hill whence flows the infant Blackwater.

It was known long ago as 'The Allo'; hence came Edmund Spenser's 'Swift Allo Tombling from Slew Logher Steep.'

The Loire, often called 'France's last wild river', rises in the yard of a farmer away to the east of the country, so modest in its birth that it flows out of a wooden pit.

That lucky peasant's yard is a famous place of pilgrimage: the French love their rivers.

We, alas, do not. How many people could tell you the source of the Dodder or the Camac – or even of the Liffey itself?

I have never heard of anyone going to see the source of

the Blackwater, even though people with a gift for exaggeration have been known to call it 'the Irish Rhine'.

Nevertheless, Sliabh Luachra continues to expand. It now embraces a considerable expanse of territory along by the Kerry–Cork border and is expanding rapidly into both counties.

Whence this wondrous transformation?

The answer to most mysteries is simple: Sliabh Luachra's growth corresponds to the growth of what is loosely called traditional music.

There was a time – and it isn't very long ago – when traditional music was distinctly unfashionable.

Segovia, almost on his own, brought respectability to the music of the Spanish gypsies.

The civil-rights movement in the United States was the catalyst of the folk revival we have experienced in this generation.

And thus the singers and musicians of the country around Sliabh Luachra found a much wider audience than ever they could have envisaged.

Their songs and their music had been associated with the Ireland of hardship and poverty. So too had the Gaelic language: this was among the reasons for its decline.

The revolution – if such it was – brought a new awareness. Sliabh Luachra now symbolises a cultural cornucopia.

Its boundaries may not be well defined – or indeed defined at all – but two solid statements can be made about it: Sliabh Luachra is mostly hill-country – and it is a great area for songs and music.

I have written before about its musicians – and especially the ones I knew best. They were Patrick Keeffe and Denis

Murphy and Jerry McCarthy – fiddlers three – and the famous accordion player Johnny Leary.

In the current number of *Sliabh Luachra*, a lively and scholarly annual now on its fifth journey, the emphasis is on the songs.

Christie Cronin, a modest son of Gneeveguilla, contributes a lovely essay entitled 'My Life and Music'.

Christie is a noted singer and tells us how the seed fell and how it grew.

He was only about five when the singing at the monthly Holy Hour enthralled him.

It was Gregorian chant – and Christie quickly learned 'O Salutaris' and 'Tantum Ergo'.

His father did nothing to discourage him: he too was a singer, but in a less exalted mode.

Christie makes no attempt to define 'traditional' or 'folk', but it is clear that his attitude to these terms is liberal.

He includes, for instance, 'The Headford Ambush' in his collection.

That took place as recently as 1921 – but tradition, I suppose, must begin somewhere.

Christie's mother played the fiddle but she had only one song: it began, 'There came into this village green a soldier from the war.'

For some strange reason, it is seldom that you will meet a fiddler who has many songs or indeed any songs at all.

Patrick Keeffe had only one song: 'My heart is broken from the oul' black saucepan that makes the dip.' It wasn't a classic.

Christie Cronin tells about his first experience on the stage: he rendered 'There's a dear little isle in the western ocean.'

Thence he progressed to the Fleadh Cheoil in Kilgarvan:

'I was fasinated by the different styles . . . I was delighted to be part of the occasion, even though I didn't win.'

He goes on: 'What first attracts me to a song is the air; then I try to ornament it.'

He adds: 'The hallmark of a good *sean-nós* singer is that he or she will never sing the same way twice.' I agree.

And I like this: 'What I enjoy greatly is a session with four or five people, each giving a song in turn. Thar's what it's all about.'

We read in another article about John Brosnan, the famous tailor of Scartaglen.

When he finished his travels as a journeyman, he settled down at home and founded the Scartaglen Fife and Drum Band.

It consisted of twenty-eight flutes, three drums and a triangle. Nevertheless, it lasted only two years: political differences intervened.

In *Sliabh Luachra* you can read too about the famous annual race meeting at Knocknagree.

As one who was deeply involved long ago in this esoteric branch of sport, I was greatly interested.

And such names as Little Mo and Inishshannon Lass and Little Breeze were to me like music heard from afar.

The author of the piece, Dan Moynihan, tells about an occasion long ago when it seemed that the meeting would have to be abandoned.

The weather was the culprit: 'It rained so much that there was no hope of carrying on. Novenas, prayers and pious aspirations seemed to be to no avail.'

The meeting could hardly be postponed until the following day – it was the Sabbath.

In great trepidation, a deputation went to the parish priest, Canon Brosnan.

The good man knew that the venture had cost a lot of time, effort and money: he gave the meeting his blessing.

Next day the sun came out gloriously: 'Crowds flocked in from all quarters.' The occasion was a mighty success.

And so there was Sunday racing in the country long before it came to Leopardstown and other fashionable venues.

Incidentally, the contractor who annually erected the temporary stand for Knocknagree races was a native of Auckland.

He was a certain Dan Dennehy. He had played for the All Blacks – and coached them.

Knocknagree races, as far as I know, are no more; it was a big meeting in its heyday.

I could name some well-known 'under-the-rules' jockeys who rode there but they wouldn't thank me for it.

There is a dimension to Sliabh Luachra which I need hardly mention; it is a great place for verbal artistry.

When I tell you that Éamon Kelly is a native son, I need hardly say much more; incidentally, he has a nice piece in the current number.

Whence came this especial love of music, song and language?

It is common in people who live in the hills; music especially is their anodyne.

It is a long story and we will let the fox and the hare and the rabbit sit until another day.

Evening Press, 14 November 1989

Football Mania
A Global Affliction

Donal Corcoran, an aficionado who is devoted to Sligo Rovers and Liverpool in that order, told me a strange story the other night.

We were in Anfield's Main Stand awaiting the momentous clash of the home team and Arsenal.

He had been there too on the previous Tuesday night when Liverpool's 5–1 defeat of West Ham consigned the London club to the First Division.

He travelled back to London on a train crowded with West Ham supporters – and therein lies the little tale.

Donal knows more than most about the depth of Football passion – not for nothing did he grow up in Sligo – but he was amazed at the aftermath of West Ham's defeat.

There wasn't much talk on that train to Euston or much drinking: the journey gave the word 'muted' an extra dimension.

Instead there was much weeping and even sobbing – and it wasn't confined to women and children.

Strong men cried unashamedly; Donal could hardly believe his eyes and ears.

I shouldn't have been surprised: I have been acquainted with Football in England long enough to know that for a great many people there it is much more than a game.

We all know people who are devoted to counties and

clubs here at home, but it isn't the same kind of devotion.

Ireland is still in the main composed of rooted societies; even Dublin remains a cluster of villages.

The same was once true of London and the other English cities but it is much less so now.

And this, I believe, is the main reason for devotion to a Football club reaching intensity which we do not know.

Where a social unit has no clearly defined geographical basis, the club becomes the extended family.

Of course there are people here who have a similar intensity of devotion. I know men of no great affluence who went over for Bill Shankly's funeral – but they are a minority.

I was in Anfield last Friday night and witnessed something of a kind that I have never experienced in Croke Park or Dalymount or Lansdowne Road.

Next to me in the main stand was a young girl with whom I conversed in snatches during the game.

She was a bright lass and for good measure possessed the kind of common sense that seems a monopoly of Lancashire.

And yet at about two minutes past ten she uttered a frightening scream and put her elbows on her knees and her head in her hands and wept and sobbed.

The reaction seemed wildly incommensurate with the cause: a young man named Michael Thomas had just scored a goal that almost certainly would cost Liverpool the Championship.

On the way out from the stadium I met a man who said to me, 'The referee should be shot. That first goal wasn't a goal at all.'

And I was reminded of a story told about the late lamented Leslie Compton.

Leslie, as my generation will remember, was a 'stopper' centre-back for Arsenal who looked on a score against his side as a grievous reflection on himself.

And you can imagine his chagrin when Tottenham Hotspur won the local derby with a score in the last minute.

He ran to the referee and said, 'That wasn't a goal.'

Arbiters, contrary to repeated rumours, are not without a sense of humour: the man in black said, 'Les, buy the *Star* on your way home and you'll find out.'

The man who said to me that Alan Smith's goal was invalid is an old and dear friend who has built up a very successful business.

In matters arising out of the real world, I would always listen with great care to his opinions.

And here he was on a balmy May night denying the evidence of my senses.

If you are acquainted with Liverpool's home ground, you will know that Seat 280 in the main stand gives you an excellent view of the goal area at the Anfield end.

And I had seen nothing suspicious about Arsenal's first score, but I said to my friend, 'I agree.' It wasn't an occasion for proclaiming the truth from the rooftops.

Believe me, there are people for whom such a calamitous defeat as Liverpool suffered on Friday night is akin to a death in the family.

And in some instances it is literally true: after Brazil were kicked out of the 1966 World Cup finals by their Portuguese cousins, twenty-seven suicides back at home were linked to the disaster.

And after West Germany had lost in the final that year, a young man who lived in a Bavarian village and was deemed to be a paragon of sense went to his bedroom and shot himself dead.

I doubt if anyone in this country would react so extremely, though I know a few small boys who came back from Liverpool last Friday night convinced that the sun would never rise again.

In the last ten years or so, a new element has infiltrated our culture.

Fathers take their small boys to matches in Britain – or perhaps, such is the current economic climate, it is the other way round.

Whatever the situation, it is healthy and it is a wonderful change: in my boyhood we thought we were doing very well if we got to a match in Tralee or Killarney.

And of course the proliferation of Soccer in this island is about the best thing that happened to us since the arrival of the potato.

Soccer is the most democratic of all field games in that it has room for the big and the small and for those not particularly gifted with basic speed.

Young lads now in every corner of the island have a choice of games: it isn't too long since they had a 'choice' of one. And choice is an element of freedom.

It would be hard to exaggerate the influence of the GAA in our society, but not all that influence has been for the best.

Hurling is a splendid game, and Gaelic Football could be; where the Association sinned was in promulgating a synthetic culture.

It isn't long since every village had its Joe McCarthy – a big mouth who looked on himself as the great Gael. There are still a few around.

The infamous Ban was rooted in mesmerising ignorance: it has gone from the rule book but it is still lurking around.

It is an astonishing fact that now on the run-in to the twenty-first century we still have people in our midst who are convinced that if you play Rugby or Soccer you are an inferior Irishman.

Not least of the irony inherent in this is that Rugby was once the national game – as much a part of our culture as bacon and spuds and cabbage and the clay pipe.

This can be proven as satisfactorily as a mathematical proposition, but the old guard do not wish to know.

They still believe that it matters what game you play. The great Gael can be a usurer or a slum landlord: all that counts is that he plays or follows the right games.

This attitude is diminishing; we are inching our way towards freedom.

And of course we are becoming more acquainted with mainland Europe: the Summer of 1988 in West Germany will for many an Irish person be a golden memory.

And it opened the senses of many who had until then been indifferent to Football and perhaps to all forms of sport.

I don't mind someone not being interested in sport; the annoying aspect is that such people tend to boast about their indifference.

They seem to regard it as a symptom of intellectual superiority. Anyone who works in the sports department of a newspaper can confirm that this strange attitude exists.

And of course the implication is that all aficionados are intellectually inferior.

My old friend Brendan Kennelly finds this attitude less annoying than amusing: in his modest way he is a kind of Renaissance man.

About the same Brendan there is a famous story which is absolutely authentic.

One evening in the dear live days not quite beyond recall, he was playing for his native Ballylongford against Daugh in the final of the North Kerry League – and therein lies the tale.

In the last minute he pointed a fifty that won the game.

In the pub that night he was approached by a veteran peasant who said: 'Are you Brendan Kennelly the poet?'

Brendan confessed, and the veteran said, 'By gor, for a poet you've a great belt of a ball.'

I need hardly add that Soccer in this part of our island is now enjoying a high noon.

And I wouldn't be surprised to discover that there are people so happily innocent of politics that they believe Jack Charlton is the Anglo-Irish Agreement.

Evening Press, 30 May 1989

HOPKINS AND VAN GOGH
PUSHING BACK THE BOUNDS

'At the Wedding March' is not among the better-known poems of Gerard Manley Hopkins but it embodies most of his virtues:

> *God with honour hang your head,*
> *Groom, and grace you, bride your bed*
> *With lissom scions, sweet scions,*
> *Out of hallowed bodies bred.*
>
> *Each be other's comfort kind:*
> *Deep, deeper than divined,*
> *Divine charity, dear charity,*
> *Fast you ever, fast bind.*
>
> *Then let the March tread our ears:*
> *I to him turn with tears*
> *Who to wedlock, his wonder wedlock,*
> *Does triumph and immortal years.*

The reader whose first encounter with Hopkins was through this poem might recoil and utter such judgements as 'Obscure', 'Pretentious' and 'Self-indulgent'.

He would be justified – up to a point. Hopkins needs knowing. It isn't a difficult process; and when it is complete, more or less, the newcomer will find very little obscurity in

132

his work, no pretentiousness and only a modicum of self-indulgence.

The matrix of 'At the Wedding March' – as of all his poetry – is Hopkins's abiding intuition that the universe is purposeful.

Nominally he was a Catholic – indeed for most of his adult life he was a scrupulously obedient member of the Jesuit order – but his sense of the world seems to be too all-embracing to be confined within the walls of any doctrine.

I have long thought of him as the Vincent Van Gogh of poetry. The comparison may seem pretentious; so be it.

Van Gogh too was profoundly religious, but hardly in an orthodox way. His compassion resembled that of Hopkins: it overflowed the parameters of theology.

And as artists they had much in common – above all, a fierce ambition to speak for themselves, in modes of their own.

Van Gogh was born in 1853 and died in 1890; Hopkins was born in 1844 and died in 1889. Thus they were close contemporaries.

Their deaths were not dissimilar.

Van Gogh, contrary to popular belief, didn't commit suicide. In a cry for help, he shot himself. The wound was not in itself fatal – but so poor was his condition that it led to his death.

One of Hopkins's last poems, 'Thou Art Indeed Just, Lord', indicates an extreme state of depression; it recalls William Cowper's 'The Castaway'.

The medical details of his last days are rather vague; it is hard not to suspect that he had lost the will to live.

It seems incredible that two such marvellous artists

should be sunk in despair at a time of their lives when they could have been looking towards a harvest of appreciation.

Hopkins and Van Gogh cannot but have known that they were great; seemingly this knowledge didn't suffice.

In one of his last letters to his brother Theo, we find Van Gogh complaining of a sadness 'which I cannot understand'.

And in a letter written to his great friend, the poet Robert Bridges, in the October of 1888, Hopkins refers to Autumn: 'If all were seen, fallen leaves of my poor life between all the leaves of it.'

The explanation for his depression and that of Van Gogh seems clear: neither got the appreciation for which he hungered.

Hopkins's poetry was not published in his lifetime, due to the regulations of his order.

And if the ban had been lifted, it is likely that he would have suffered rebuff and humiliation, as Van Gogh did.

To us now it seems incredible that the Impressionist painters should have been so misunderstood and reviled, but we are judging with the help of a century's advancement.

Conservatism is a force that should never be under-estimated – and professional critics tend to be arch exponents of it.

It is most unlikely that Hopkins's poetry would have been critically acclaimed – if it came to be published at all.

Its boldness might have made it seem not only revolutionary but iconoclastic.

There was nothing to prevent Van Gogh from exhibiting his work. Little good it did him: it was only in his last few years that mites of appreciation came his way, mostly from fellow painters.

It wasn't as if Van Gogh had set out to assault convention. He was anything but a conscious rebel; he was steeped in traditional painting – and greatly respected it.

Hopkins too was a deep student of mainstream literature; it wasn't a coincidence that he became a teacher of Latin and Greek.

Neither could be termed a primitive; both worked unremittingly at their craft; both were great theorists, as you will see from their notes and letters.

And as Hopkins sensed that the language of English lyrical poetry had reached its pinnacle in the mid-nineteenth century, so Van Gogh felt that 'classical' painting had a set of conventions that restricted his expression.

W. H. Gardner in his introduction to the collected poems of Hopkins writes that he led poetry forward by taking it back.

In other words, he broke away from outworn conventions and worked back towards English as it is spoken.

In this ambition, he wasn't a pioneer. William Wordsworth envisioned a similar goal, but his radicalism was confined to theme and vocabulary; Hopkins set out to create a prosody that would be his own.

Some of his theorising goes a bit too far. Let us be honest about it: few people, despite the arguments of the purists, read poetry aloud; they say it to the mind's ear.

And when Hopkins puts stress-marks over some syllables, he is being fussy. They add nothing; we all tend to read in our own way.

It is a minor fault and would probably have been erased if he had been more in touch with the public.

Thomas Hardy, that shrewdest of craftsmen – and,

incidentally, Hopkins's contemporary, only that he outlived him by almost thirty years – allowed his words to live in their own music.

Hopkins wrote at great length about the theory of poetry, and his manuscripts are like battlefields, so many are the corrections.

And of course distillation is the name of the game – and yet at the end of that famous day you think of Ezra Pound: 'There are no rules for writing poetry; there is only the music of the line.'

Of course that is an extreme statement but it points towards a truth.

And once again we are back to Croce's comment on Shelley.

He was talking about the view that Shelley had great thoughts which he couldn't express – and said: 'There is no thought until the mental impulse is put into words.'

I cannot help suspecting that, despite all Hopkins's theorising about prosody, his mental impulses had their own rhythms.

His genius lies in his felicitous use of words.

You are tempted to say that he resurrected the English language.

Words that had fallen out of use came singing back.

And words that were unfashionable in mainstream poetry were promoted.

Again there is a comparison with Van Gogh. In a letter to his brother Theo he said: 'How important is it to know how to mix on the palette those colours which have no name and yet are the real foundation of everything.'

Let us return to the little poem 'At the Wedding March'.

It needs a second reading – and perhaps a third – and yet it is easily understood once you come to terms with the use of language.

You will see Hopkins in a more expansive mood in 'Binsey Poplars'.

The first of its three stanzas seems – at least to me – to take words, as Ernest Hemingway used to say, from algebra into calculus:

> *My aspens dear, whose airy cages quelled,*
> *Quelled or quenched in leaves the leaping sun,*
> *All felled, felled, are all felled;*
> *Of a fresh and following folded rank*
> *No spared, not one*
> *That dandalled a sandaled*
> *Shadow that swam or sank*
> *On meadow and river and wind-*
> *wandering weed-winding bank.*

I suppose we all have our mantras; they aren't necessarily little phrases.

Mine include several of Hopkins's poems and several of Van Gogh's paintings.

They have put us immensely in their debt by revealing the infinity of the world's wonder.

Hopkins, incidentally, died in Dublin and, as far as I know, is buried in the Jesuits' plot in Glasnevin.

Van Gogh died in a little town called Auvers-sur-Oise in northern France and, as Theo wrote, ' He sleeps amidst the cornfields.'

Evening Press, 19 September 1989

The Romance of the Turf

'Twas in the year of 'thirty-nine
And the sky was full of lead.
Hitler was going for Danzig
And Paddy for Holyhead.
And foundations they were cracking
And the roofs all falling in
And McAlpine was searching Liverpool
To find the Darky Finn.

And in that same year a bookmaker came to our town, rented a shop, put a lovely fair-haired girl behind the counter and the words 'Turf Accountant' on the window.

And on the day after he had opened, an old man from the mountain came in and said to the bemused blonde, 'I have a grand rick for sale. Every sod as hard and as black as coal. And as dry as snuff. How much a ton would you be giving?'

These were the days of the great turf rush and the moorland between Castle Island and Listowel was its Klondike. And just as bank clerks and shop assistants went on the trail of '98, so did the most unlikely people take to the mountain during Hitler's war.

In those vanished and yet present Summers, Football was a minor theme. Rommel, Montgomery and Stalingrad superseded Moclair, Keohane and Croke Park. And the turf superseded them all. It was, as every pub wit in the country said, the burning topic.

Men who before the invasion of Poland had never handled a slean or pike now became imbued with the fanaticism of converts. And they would return every evening with wondrous tales of what had happened up in the mountain.

They were finding themselves. They were suddenly cast back into the primal world. They had come to know the supreme crisis of trying to light a fire on a misty day and to delight in the first signs of steam from the kettle.

Suddenly Football was seen in its proper light. It was a fascinating diversion – but the cutting and saving of the turf was a stern game. And the term 'great man' took on a new meaning. Before, it had signified an eminent foot-baller – a Stack or a Brosnan or a Landers. Now it was used about men whose prowess in the skills of the bog made them modest kings, as sought after as fiddlers on St Brigid's Night.

And most in demand of all were the expert sleansmen. They were treated with the deference that Football managers show to a youngster who is regularly firing in goals for some team in the Fourth Division.

The sleansman is both manager and captain. He dictates the pace and the tactics, and unless he is wise as well as skilled can make life difficult for the rest of the team.

Turf cutting is very much a team game. When all are skilled and sensitive, it can be a pleasure; when one of the team is an egoist it can be torture. And it is the sleansman, most of all, who can make or break.

The breencher is the navvy of turf cutting. He impales

the sods on a three-pronged pike and despatches them out to the man on the bank, known as the spreader, whose task is to lay them out in regular rows.

He also is armed with a three-pronged pike and, though his work is light in the sense of muscular effort, he needs a good eye and a sense of mathematics: he has to make an intuitive equation between volume and area.

The spreader is usually a lad in his apprenticeship to bogcraft or a veteran who has borne the heat and the weight of many Summers and is now a kind of emeritus professor.

The breenchers are the heavy brigade, and in past generations they were distinguished by their wrist-straps as matadors are by their pigtails. Their work looks simple – but here, as in many fields, appearances are woefully deceptive. To graduate as a breencher of the first division, you need the strength and stamina of a second-row forward and something of the skill of a scrum-half. Accuracy of pitching and length of delivery are essential.

And the sod must land in such a way that it is not broken. And the muscular energy expended is far greater than meets the eye of the casual observer. The wrist-straps are not altogether for show.

In a typical day's work, the breencher shifts about twenty tons of peat an average of about fifteen feet in distance and three in height. Such a feat entitles you to be at least a private, first class, in McAlpine's Fusiliers.

A Belgian who married an Irish governess and came to live in our town summarised the work division in the turf cutting in a way that has become part of local lore. He had hired three men and went up to the mountains in the afternoon with a jar of stout.

Before they sat down to partake of it, he watched them finishing a section. And as they rested, he was asked by the sleansman what he thought of the operation. The answer was a classic in work study.

'The sleansman,' he said, 'has only to point his cutter at it. The bank manager has only to share it out. But the breencher should be relieved every half-hour.' Which, as Éamon Kelly would say, he should.

The other aristocrats of the moorland are the guide and the clamper. The latter is the maker of the rick, whose skills not only give the pile of dry sods a functional shape but who also takes pride in its appearance.

He is not only concerned with waterproofing, with 'keeping out the drop', but with the creation of mathematical beauty. Many a time we have seen a clamper eye his finished work with the satisfaction that Manet knew when he looked at his *Girl in the Bar of the Folies-Bergère*.

The clamper is less in demand now: plastic has affected him as it did the sackmakers of Pakistan. But even in the age of the tractor, the guide is still an important man. Country people use words punctiliously – and he is not called a guide for nothing.

There are places too soft or rough or narrow for a tractor, and the guide's task is to steer his horse so wisely that he will not sink or fall down. Sometimes one needs hands as sensitive as Lester Piggott's and to know as much about the going as Tony Power.

Ah, yes, the cutting and saving of turf is a stern game. It demands skill and character. In a season in the bog, you will see a man's inner being revealed as surely as you would in Dalymount or Croke Park or Lansdowne Road.

We had a friend long ago who used to say: 'The only way to get your turf is to fight it all the way.' And again it is not for nothing that the implements used in the bog – the spade and slean and pike and hay knife – are always called weapons.

And we are glad that the bogs are alive again. King Coal is depleted and King Oil is playing hard to get. We put our trust in the turf – the once and future king.

Evening Press

We talk of a writer's style. But has an honest writer a style at all? It is true that there are little habits that make some easy to distinguish. But in the larger sense of rhythm and vocabulary and syntax, is not a distinctive style perhaps a weakness? Of modern writers, Hemingway best illustrates this possibility.

One hears of his famous economy. But it is a dubious economy that takes a hundred words to tell you that a man ordered a glass of beer, got it and drank it. We hear too of his idiomatic language and his clean line. But surely there are times when neither is suited to what you want to say.

The serenity of Manet demands a different language from the tortured visions of Van Gogh. William Faulkner could write as clean a line as any. The famous lifting of the log in 'Pantaloon in Black' is a classic of orthodox prose, but sometimes he is clumsy, repetitive, rhetorical, almost incoherent – because he is attempting total expression of what is almost inexpressible.

Hemingway would attempt to capture a railway station in the same way as he would attempt to express a storm: the famous style tends to transmute all it touches into its own texture. It falsifies. At the heart of this is not, one feels, a lack of perception, but a lack of honesty, or courage.

'My opinions have been called singular; they are merely sincere. I say what I think. I think what I feel. I cannot help receiving certain impressions from things, and I have sufficient courage to declare what they are. This is the only singularity I am conscious of.' The words are William Hazlitt's, and they are characteristic.

Yes, he received certain impressions from things and had sufficient courage to declare what they were. Is there a better fingerpost towards a definition of the artist? And it is the 'sufficient' courage that makes it so right and splendid. About Hazlitt there was a marvellous wholeness; the essence of this lies in having that 'sufficient courage'.

In his famous essay on the fight between Thomas Hickman and Bill Neate, there is a telling little passage. At his inn on the morning after that immortal battle he observed his travelling companion reading now and then from a pocket volume and is delighted to see that it is Rousseau's novel, *La Nouvelle Heloise*.

Hazlitt's comment is: 'Ladies, after this will you contend that a love for the Fancy is incompatible with the culti-vation of sentiment?' The question is addressed to more than the ladies. Hazlitt is one of the very few English writers to have taken a passionate interest in sport, and in that little passage there is a hint of self-defence.

An American writer would hardly have asked such a question: sport is deeply interwoven through their litera-ture: a reflection, perhaps, of the fact that the frontier mentality survives. There are English writers who have interested themselves in the sports of the masses, but they are mostly dabblers. They lack what the Spanish call *aficion*.

Hazlitt would have none of such people. In *The Fight*, he refers to those returning from the battle who interrupt his philosophic leisure in the inn as 'not real fancy-men but interlopers'. This is the valid contempt of the true lover of the Fancy for the vulgar. They went for the occasion; he went for the fight.

Why did Boxing so fascinate him? Part of the answer is in what Joe Louis said: 'In the ring you can run but you cannot hide.' It is no place for pretence. Its truths are fiercely objective – in hardly any other setting is your essential self so sternly searched out.

Hazlitt admired the protagonists of the Fancy for their honesty and courage. Boxing in his day was an even more unrelenting appraisal than it is now: the fight went on until one or other of the contestants was knocked out. The drama you see on a stage is, after all, make-believe. Hamlet rises intact at the final curtain; for the pugilist there is no such reprieve.

The fight between Neate and Hickman was especially enthralling. The contrast between them was as marked in personality as in physique. Neate is big and awkward and honest; Hickman is of only average size but is beautifully made: in demeanour he is the very embodiment of cockiness.

In his prelude to the fight, Hazlitt draws the protagonists with great clarity. Hickmann is like Muhammad Ali before his time. His predictions are boastful and in colourful language. Hazlitt comments that modesty should accompany the Fancy as a shadow and that the best men were always the best-behaved. We know different now.

On his way to the ring, Hickman struts; Neate strolls along, 'his knock-knees bending under his huge bulk'. And before their coming, how conscious we are of the apprehension.

'This is the trying time. It is the time the heart sickens, as you think what the two champions are about and how short a time will determine their fate.'

And how simply the scene is painted. It is December: 'The grass is wet and the ground miry and ploughed up with multitudinous feet, except that within the ring itself there was a spot of virgin-green closed in and unprofaned by vulgar tread that shone with dazzling brightness in the midday sun.'

We are there with Hazlitt in that great crowd on the midwinter noon of more than a hundred and fifty years ago.

Soon the waiting will be over. And 'after the first blow is struck, there is no opportunity for nervous apprehension – swallowed up in the immediate interest of the scene.'

The battle itself is a classic example of boxer against fighter. It might be Corbett against Sullivan, only that this time it is the boxer who is vanquished. Hazlitt lets you know the winner long before the fight starts: there was little point in concealing the fact, since it was already well known to his readers.

Organised Football was unknown then. Boxing and Racing carried an enormous weight of interest. On that day when Neate and Hickman did battle, one feels that everybody who could was there and that the rest were there in spirit. Only the Epsom Derby and the Aintree Grand National now create similar excitement.

Hazlitt's purpose in hs account of the fight is not to keep you in suspense wondering who is going to win but to delineate the ebb and flow of the battle. At first it is Hickman who dominates. He is light, vigorous, elastic: he strikes Neate five blows in as many seconds. He seems to hold a sword directed against an unarmed body.

But Neate is not cowed, only particularly cautious. Hazlitt sees him clench his teeth and knit his brows against the sun. He changes his method of fighting and frustrates

Hickman's lightning advances. Hickman, rather like Carpentier against Dempsey, risks all on one mighty blow. He misses – and takes a mighty blow instead.

From that moment, the balance of power is gone. It is not now a question of who will win, but how long Hickman will survive. And the remarkable thing about him is that, for all his vainglory, he is a man of infinite courage. Again one is reminded of Muhammad Ali and how in his first fight with Frazier he bore humiliation manfully.

Hickman, like Ali, might have been dashed in his opinion of himself: 'It was the first time he had ever been so punished.' But his courage is undiminished and the end comes only when he is beaten into unconsciousness and even his great heart cannot bring him up to the scratch.

His first words on awakening are: 'Where am I? What is the matter?' His second answers: 'Nothing is the matter. You have lost the battle, but you are the bravest man alive.' Hazlitt would widen that commendation to cover all pugilists; what he admires in the Fancy is that it leaves no room for the cowardly and the dishonest.

We are back again to 'sufficient courage'. Hazlitt had it as abundantly as Hickman. And if, compared to other writers, he has no style, it is because he knew that the essence of style is to have no style. What is being expressed dominates: the artist becomes its voice.

If Hazlitt writes with zest, it is because he lived with zest. When he was dying, he was neither particularly rich nor famous. He had known more than the ordinary measure of tribulations, yet his last words were: 'Well, I have had a happy life.' One understands.

Evening Press

A Dubbalin Man

Have no doubt about it: the heart of the country is sound. In the forenoon on Monday, a string of buses almost surrounded Store Street station, all carrying on their destination board the magic sign 'Races'. Senior citizens climbed in as excited as if making their maiden voyage to Fairyhouse.

Our immediate neighbour was a member of that remarkable species unknown to Freud, Jung and Adler; he was, in short, a Dublin man. They come no better. And, unlike mere mortals, they are ageless. The typical specimen was there when the first ford of hurdles was built across the river.

He was having a drink in a bar near the Castle that snowy Christmas night long ago when Hugh O'Donnell and his cousin got outside the walls and set off for the mountains. He was at Emmet's execution and he was in the Royal Oak the evening Burke and Cavendish were assassinated.

And he will still be there when the first flyovers attempt to make Dublin a modern city. Our neighbour yesterday was a prime specimen: friendly, articulate and bursting with a magnificent assortment of information. He gave us a great start to what was a lovely day.

Do you remember when Fairview Corner was the city boundary? We were told about it as we travelled through that strange limbo where conurbation merges raggedly into countryside. One thought of East London and Essex, where neon signs are reflected in the marshes.

But soon we were into real country: the unmistakeable proof was a flock of splendid white hens scratching and scraping and picking in a ploughed field of yellow loam. And despite the recent snows and the inclement winds, there were abundant signs of Spring's progress.

Green shoots of whitethorn coloured the hedges, and blackberry bushes were in bud. Our neighbour was indifferent to them; perhaps he was like Dr Johnson, who said that beyond Hyde Park all else was desert. Bohemians' winning of the League was of infinitely more concern.

They were his team. 'Followed them all my life. Only once I felt like reneging – when Drums beat them in the Cup, and Drums only in the Leinster League.' As we left Dublin farther behind, the road narrowed until in the approach to Ratoath it was like a homely boreen.

Here you could see the value of shelter. The grass was greener and speckled with bright yellow. One remembered Patrick Kavanagh's 'Dandelions growing on headlands, showing their unloved hearts to everyone.'

Our neighbour was now analysing modern Soccer.

'All fancy gear is what they go in for now. And moustaches and long hair. Footballers how are you! I remember Georgie Lennox – played with Brideville. Often came straight from the building site on Saturday straight onto the field as black as a sweep. He was a footballer.'

We turn into Ratoath. Is it village or hamlet? A hamlet is a village without a pub – so Ratoath qualifies as a village. Our neighbour's analysis goes on: 'Looking at Leeds and

Ipswich the other night. All this messing around in the middle of the field – that's not Football.

'Leeds are not a great team. Ipswich played more direct – up the wings and across the field, coming out away from the keeper. That's the ball. Had a few bob on. Knew they'd win.' We are now inching along the road to the racecourse.

The double-decker bus seems incongruous in this rural lane, like a salmon that had strayed into a little stream. Our neighbour is making a Proustian journey into the past. 'Used to cycle out here long ago, a great crowd of us. Racing one another.

'Only a few bob in our pocket but we'd enjoy ourselves. Never missed a National. Prince Regent – he was the daddy of them all.' We could not agree more. The talk goes on. Shaun Peel, Jack Chaucer, Revelry, Golden Jack – the names are like music heard from afar.

As we walk up the wide path to the course we pass little groups who seem to have fled their homes and brought what they could with them. Carrier bags are bulging with giant flasks and great parcels of sandwiches and quart cider bottles full of milk.

The consumer society is in full swing. Our Dublin man has cronies to meet and we go our different ways. And we like to be alone at the races; it is not so much snobbery as dearly bought experience. Aloneness is an aid to concentration.

And eight races demand a fair share of mental energy. We have long learned the folly of wagering on every event, but this is a holiday and we feel that we have a licence to do the fool – not that we need it. Barry Brogan is in the first and we are glad to see him back in his kingdom.

We wager on his mount, Skryne. He is away in the style

of Out and About, and across Ballyhack seems like a fox before hounds. As he comes down the hill, the bullocks in a neighbouring field run lazily away. Across the fence, seven tractors are drawing harrows, freshly browning the yellow soil.

The attendant multitude of seagulls are unbothered by this sudden galloping of horses. They go on with their work as the field turns into the straight where Skryne is challenged and mastered by the unfancied Possible. Somebody says: 'He has them all slaughtered – except one.'

In the next we again back not so much a horse as a jockey. Michael Morris justifies our faith – and at a good price. For the third race we get a welter of information, all genuine. At least seven horses are home and dried; in a rare moment of wisdom we opt out and go to look at the 'outside'.

We are back in the world of Munster flapping. On the white-clothed tables are pyramids of oranges and apples; the swinging boats and their intrepid sailors make ancient rhythms in the air; ice cream and chips are consumed in quantities that must gladden the hearts of the Irish Farmers' Association.

For one glorious afternoon, the Big Rock Candy Mountain springs in a Meath field. While we are in its ambience, we watch the third race. Sand Pit, our own original fancy, wins handily – without a shilling of our money. In our mind's ear we hear the voice of Burl Ives: 'When will we ever learn?'

In the fourth, Ballywilliam Boy is giving away lumps of weight – and, as they say in the racing freemasonry, weight can stop a train. But we have old faith in Sleator's judgement and put our money on this son of Sayajirao. Do you remember him, full brother to the immortal Dante?

Ballywilliam Boy is always well in touch and comes with a nicely timed run to win comfortably. There is an unscheduled paragraph of excitement as three riderless horses gallop through the children who have infiltrated onto the track.

Next year these errant juveniles should be rounded up for their protection and incarcerated until racing is over in a tent well stocked with chips and ice cream and copies of the *Beano*.

The expectation preceding the big race is palpable. The parade ring is deeply surrounded: Captain Christy is the observed of all observers. Out of old loyalty we have a little bet on him, remembering his great youthful deeds in Tralee and Listowel. Our wager of the day is on Brown Lad: form and information leave little choice.

As the horses go down, the rooftop stand is as crowded as a refugee ship. Alas, there is no duel. The Captain, the new Playboy of the Western World, is soon affording Bobby Coonan no more than a distant view. Despite all the mingled shoutings, it is obviously Brown Lad bar a fall.

Tommy Carberry smiles as he comes away from the last fencel; it is his first National. We are now well ahead. Three races remain – and the rest in silence. We will say no more than that we used out licence to do the fool. At the end, the balance of payments has levelled.

The rooks are returning as we walk down to the road. Little streams of people are going home across the fields. Our Dubbalin man is not with us on the way back; he is on some other bus, doubtless explaining the vagaries of the Captain.

Next to us, a small boy is asleep on his mother's lap. The solid happenings of the day are already dissolving into dreams.

Evening Press, April 1975

Games People Play

'Someone is knocking at the door –
Mother come down and see!'
'I'm sure it's naught but a beggar –
Tell him I'm busy.'

It was not a beggar but a messenger from the colliery to say that the man of the house had been injured. That is the opening of a poem D. H. Lawrence wrote when he was very young.

He never worked 'down pit' himself – and yet possibly better than anyone else he expressed the miner's world. He grew up in a colliery village; from his father he imbibed the essence of the life that went on below.

In Winter the miners saw daylight only at weekends. They went down in the dark and came up in the dark. And they had an especially sharp awareness of the countryside because they were so much away from it; Lawrence inherited that.

It has been said that he could describe people in a field – and that you would remember the field when you had forgotten the people.

There are jobs that dull the brain and deaden the spirit; coal-mining is not among them. It demands great sharpness of mind and body; it is no trade for the indifferent.

Today it is less dirty than once it was, but it is still

arduous and dangerous; in Lawrence's childhood it was far more so. Then it was all muscle power – and pitfalls and explosions were more frequent.

But danger breeds awareness; and where life depends on courage and hardihood and cooperation, there is pride and dignity and a sense of community. Lawrence was lucky in his background and he lost a great deal when he cut himself away from it.

Such a world breeds a love of games that require courage and hardihood too; it is no accident that Rugby and Boxing are so much part of the miner's life.

In Lawrence's youth, Rugby was only just beginning to grow. His father and his fellow-miners hardly knew it; Nottingham was Soccer country – and there is a lovely story of his about a group of miners going across the fields to the city to see one of their comrades play with County.

The midlands is still great Soccer country but in the northern coalfields Rugby dominates – generally the League form of the game. It seems remarkable that a code of Football that grew in the public schools should take root in so different a soil. But it is not remarkable at all.

Rugby is only a more sophisticated version of the old ball-carrying games that were common throughout Britain and Ireland for centuries before modern transport, especially the train, led to more widespread competition – and codification followed.

The old form was violent and chaotic; it exists now only in a few survivals that have become more rites than competitions. The Eton Wall Game is the best-known of them.

The 'pitch' here is a long path five yards wide; the object is to force the ball to the end of the opponents' territory. A score is very rare: about one in twenty-five years is the average.

'Caid', the most popular ball game in many parts of Ireland before Cusack invented 'Gaelic' Football, was essentially the same – only the pitch might be a whole townland or even a parish.

Caid and the ball-carrying games of Britain served the same purpose: they were a crude means of expressing impulses that would otherwise have found less desirable outlets.

Rugby took deep root among the miners because, more than any other field game, it demands the total man; it is of all games the nearest to battle.

More than any other game, it satisfies the need for glory – not glory in the sense of fame or tangible honours but in the testing of your manhood and finding it not wanting.

Arduous and dangerous work especially breeds that need for glory: it creates an impulse very akin to that of art.

Rugby proved a great mould for such an impulse: it provides scope for passionate physical expression. Cusack made a mistake when he decided to 'invent' Gaelic Football.

He wished, of course, to create a distinctive game. He was being carried along on a rising tide of hysterical nationalism, but he based his invention on Soccer, a game that was hardly the natural expression of the Ireland he knew.

Soccer is above all the game of the factory worker. It is popular in the countryside in many parts, but its heartland has always been the great industrial city.

Some day some great philosopher will rise up and analyse

the relation between games, nations and social groups; in the meantime we will venture to say that there is a bond between Soccer and the machine age.

The factory worker sees in its ordered skills some reflection of his own life. It is, if you like, his art. J. B. Priestley wrote very well about that aspect long ago.

He captured the world where minds all week at lathe and capstan are kept green by looking back or forward to Saturday afternoon, when so much of their own lives is seen in a kind of distillation.

Cusack's mistake was to think that culture is something you can impose on people. You cannot: it must spring from themselves. Gaelic Football was not a good mould for expressing what one might call the Irish nature.

It has always been staggering between the stools of the carrying game and the propelling game; that is the root of its troubles. It is – and we feel sad to have to say it – a synthetic game.

It could with intelligent rules be transformed into the greatest field game of all – but that dream seems a very long way from fulfilment.

We have said that Cusack's creation did not provide a good mould for the impulses seeking expression, but Ireland is very changed now and a radically reformed Gaelic Football could be as 'national' a game as you could desire.

In Cusack's day the generality of the Irish were accustomed to labour so arduous that in their minds; in their games they sought a mould for legitimate passion.

That Ireland of epic hand labour is almost gone: we have to a considerable degree become children of the machine age too.

What we have tried to say here about games and the people that play them is no more than a fumbling attempt at a very delicate and complex question.

What we are trying to say is that sometimes you can trace a relationship between work and play. Essentially we are talking about culture.

D. H. Lawrence spoke about impulses that come up from the very earth. Such words seem mystical: they are as mystical as bread or beer or coal.

Evening Press

While the Wheel Spins

Among the gifts we received at Christmas was Peter Arnold's delightful *The Book of Gambling,* a lucid study of one of man's oldest obsessions. And we use that last word after due deliberation.

The word 'gambler' is often loosely used or is applied to victims who are only slightly smitten. And we all in our melodramatic moments tend to cast ourselves in this desperate role. But the true gambler is very rare.

Very few bookmakers, for instance, are gamblers: they operate in a field where the odds are in their favour and where there is little danger of sudden ruin. And most punters are not gamblers, though from their own experiences they can get insights into the gambler's mentality. The gambler is he whose life is dominated by the belief that he has a kind of magical knowledge of the future and that he can turn it to his account. And if that knowledge often fails him, he is nonetheless convinced.

Even modest punters know that feeling. A bad day at the races induces depression at first; often this is succeeded by a kind of oceanic state in which you are confident that the day's failure is merely the prelude to future gain.

You even feel that failure has made you sharper and less fallible and that you have only to avoid repeating the day's mistakes and you will have found the magic formula.

Dostoevsky, the great Russian writer, has analysed that

mentality in *The Gambler,* a novel that is mainly auto-biographical. Its hero is tempted into gambling by the need to make money – and is quickly obsessed.

At first he is oppressed by the sordidness of the casino and the terrible seriousness with which its denizens concentrate on the spin of the ball and wheel, but as soon as he begins to win, he experiences that strange feeling of magical power that even modest punters know.

Then he has a losing run – but by now he has acquired the gambler's sense of infallibility and is convinced of eventual success. He begins to bet wildly and loses all. This disaster is followed by a tremendous sense of excitement.

It is not easy to explain why anyone should be excited at losing a significant sum of money, but it is one of the marks of the gambler.

Some psychologists try to explain it by postulating that the gambler is unconsciously desirous of losing all he has – that he desires the kind of manic freedom that absence of worldly goods may bring.

The theory may have some truth, but hardly enough to explain the mind of the gambler. Essentially he is a believer in luck – and regards apparent disasters as springboards to greater triumphs. And the kind of luck he believes in is akin to magic.

Magic is a kind of irrational power, a breaking of the ordinary laws that seem to govern the universe. And money is associated with certain social codes, especially in the Puritan ethos.

And when you can suddenly acquire it with no apparent effort, you feel you have broken the laws and achieved escape from the bonds that make life dull and constricting.

And losing has the magic of similarly dramatic change.

And it is easy to understand why two of the most potent attractions for the gambler are horse racing and roulette.

Both are visually dramatic. But there is more to it than that. You think of the horse you have backed almost as if it were your own – and the ball in roulette falls into its resting place with the kind of finality we associate with life itself.

Roulette, of course, is the very stuff of which the romance of gambling is made. It is a purer form than horse racing, where secret knowledge can lessen the risk. Has there ever been a song about someone breaking the bookmakers on the racecourse?

But 'The Man Who Broke the Bank at Monte Carlo' swept the world. He was not, by the way, a fictitious person: Charles Wells did it in 1891, not only once, but again and again – and departed a wealthy man.

He returned some years later and lost all. During his great spell there was intense speculation about what system he was using. Before he died, a very poor man, he revealed all. The answer was simple: he had no system. He had the gambler's most potent ally, luck.

In *The Book of Gambling*, Peter Arnold analyses, among many other aspects, the mathematics of bookmakers' odds. He takes as an example a five-horse race where the odds were 7/4, 15/8, 3/1, 8/1 and 25/1. It can easily be shown that the odds here were more than 11 per cent in the bookies' favour.

In a big field they are usually larger: that same day, in a twenty-six-horse race, the bookie's advantage was almost 39 per cent. This, of course, does not prevent him from losing on individual races, but a bookie who knows his business and does not gamble has a good chance of survival.

And knowledge of mathematics is not their greatest weapon: they depend far more on knowledge of which horses are trying and which are not. Peter Arnold says: 'Considering the amount of money involved, racing is more honest than anybody could reasonably expect.' Indeed . . .

Those not in the know – and that means most of us – have to assume that all is on the level. Professional gamblers are usually able to lessen the odds against them by paying to discover the non-triers; the ordinary punter has to consider the whole field.

Peter Arnold mentions several betting systems and gives an excellent piece of advice: do not use a system until you have very thoroughly tested it and seen what logic, if any, underlies it.

He makes other good, if obvious, points: watch horses that have travelled a long distance from their stables, and remember that a jockey riding at his natural weight has an advantage over one carrying lumps of lead.

And the practice of following winning two-year-olds until they are beaten makes sense, if only because young horses generally take some time to become accustomed to the racecourse.

But the great gamblers of racing generally rely on inside knowledge – not always a sure guide. The Derby of 1844 is a case in point. That year the notorious Goodman Levi felt very confident: his entry was in reality a four-year-old called Maccabeus.

He duly won, but would hardly have done so had not Leander fallen: he was a six-year-old.

In any event, the bookmakers refused to pay; Running

Rein was disqualified, and Levi, as was customary at the time, died in poverty in France.

More successful were the conspirators who made the name Trodmore Hunt part of racing history. In 1880 they sent the fields for the Easter Monday meeting at this remote venue to the London sporting papers and duly wired in the results.

The betting shops, then illegal and therefore more vulnerable, paid out several thousand pounds. One shop queried the price of one of the winners: owing to a misprint, it appeared as 7 to 2 in one paper, whereas it was 5 to 2 in the others. And so they wrote to Trodmore.

And he found out that not only was it remote but it was not there at all. That still stands as the most ingenious coup in Racing, because it was so simple.

Its perpetrators could hardly be called gamblers – but Nico Zographos certainly could. He was the head of the famous Greek syndicate at Deauville in the 1920s. Baccarat was his speciality and it was never doubted that he was utterly honest and depended on sheer skill.

He was hardly Dostoevsky's concept of the gambler, but he at least once figured in a scene more dramatic than any in a novel. He had been losing heavily and was down to his last million francs. He risked it all in one game against two big gamblers.

The cards were dealt – two to every player. Zographos got the king of hearts and queen of spades – both valueless. His opponents were satisfied with their hands. Zographos drew his optional card. It was the nine of diamonds, the famous 'Curse of Scotland' – the best he could have drawn. Dostoevsky would not have dared to invent that.

Evening Press

Rubbing Shoulders with Royalty

He was the kind of American face you can never remember: when you try, you get an identikit somewhere between Dale Carnegie and Harry Truman.

He sat beside me on the nine o'clock flight out of Dublin on Wednesday morning – she, of course, had the window seat.

And her face too lacked individuality: you had seen her umpteen times before and would see her umpteen times again.

Their species combine an air of omniscience with an alarming ignorance: he even asked if the big race would be on television.

How little he knows of Britain: the failure to broadcast the Derby could be the first straw that would provoke a revolution.

Eager as ever to promote international goodwill, I told him the facts of life – and then blundered: I asked if they were on holiday.

He replied, 'I'm in Europe on business' – and uttered the last word with a reverence that recalled Calvin Coolidge's 'The business of America is business.'

And at that she put her finger on some invisible switch and guillotined the scintillating conversation.

And I left her to enjoy the pleasures of her window seat – and it almost broke my heart that until Northampton we were flying over a woolpack.

And I left him to contemplate his profits on the cornflakes or paper cups or whatever it is he was bringing to the grateful people of Britain.

For a dreadful moment at Heathrow I thought they were about to suggest that we share a taxi – then I would have sensed what it was like to be brought in a cart from Newgate to Tyburn.

They merely wished to know how they could get to the Penta Hotel – and we parted without kisses or embraces or vows of eternal friendship.

Outside Buckingham Palace – as predictable as the pigeons in Trafalgar Square – a patient frenzy of unashamed holidaymakers waited for a glimpse of royalty.

Many were Japanese or Germans, seemingly unembittered by the memory of a lost war. Or was it?

In their quest for a breath of the same air as the Windsors', they should have been half an hour's journey to the south – on the great rolling common known as Epsom Downs.

My interest in royalty is only marginally greater than my passion for cornflakes – and so a little happening on Wednesday confirmed my suspicion that fair play is not always an obvious element of the universe.

About a quarter past three, I left the Rubbing House – the famous pub about two furlongs north of the Derby winning post – and struggled up along the thronged walkway to get a vantage point for the great race.

I was inching along by the inside fence when, walking on the track about two lengths away from me, I saw a woman whose face was puzzlingly familiar.

She wore a coat of an alarming scarlet hue – and a matching hat with a wide brim.

And she leaned slightly forward as her high heels sank into the lush grass.

A little behind her walked a top-hatted, tail-coated retinue. And there was no mistaking the haughty, bored face of Prince Philip.

And then recognition dawned: under the wide-brimmed scarlet hat was the face familiar on the Bank of England notes.

I suppose I should have been almost dumbfounded by my nearness to a monarch – the effect, however, was very different.

As she walked along, waving and smiling diffidently to the crowd, she looked like a prisoner – irretrievably cut off from the common world.

And I thought that she could never dally at the Rubbing House and drink a pint of ale – or even half a pint – or sit under a tree on the Downs or bargain with a gypsy over the price of a sprig of white heather.

And she looked so timid and vulnerable that for a terrible moment I feared that some day she might abdicate in favour of Mrs Thatcher.

But then in a great long, gently purring car came the Queen Mother, emanating the security of one who had survived so much.

Behind was another retinue of alleged aristocrats, descendants of robber barons who had laundered their money into land and property.

But one at least looked the part: Princess Michael, blonde and beautiful and smiling, was obviously enjoying her role – and a visitor from another planet would have been confident that *she* was the Queen.

The royal procession made its way to the stands, accompanied by spatters of hand-clapping – and a muted ribaldry that might surprise those who have forgotten that not too long ago the English beheaded their king.

And then the Derby contenders came out onto the track.

And the visitor from another planet would have guessed rightly, this time, when asked to pick out the favourite.

Shergar has the clearly defined muscles of a bodybuilder, but he moves with rippling ease.

His bay coat shone. His big crooked blaze made him seem kin to the badger. You could just see the tops of his four white socks above the grass.

As they cantered past, only the faintest sound of moisture confirmed the official going: good to soft.

And now you again realised the astonishing paradox of Epsom: the world's most famous race was imminent – and scattered all over the Downs were hundreds of thousands of people who hardly cared.

Some, equipped with transistors, watched or listened; the great majority lay on the buttercupped grass, overcome by food and drink and sun.

From the vast, car-thronged infield came the eye-smiting glare of steel and glass and chrome.

The light wind from the west brought the scent of hamburgers and frying sausages and potatoes.

Down at the rails across from the winning post the crowd was densest – and radiated the sun's heat.

A pair of swallows were busy ferrying building material into the upper reaches of the stand.

They skimmed top hats with an insouciance that said: 'We were here before you – and we'll be here when you're gone.'

Away across the great horseshoe, the runners were now lining up behind the stalls – a shifting patchwork of bright colours under the dark-green canopy of beech.

Now is the time when the clock seems working to rule.

At last they are all in – except the unruly Lydia. She is banished from the race. And you wonder what would have happened if it had been Shergar.

And now the white flag is raised and the commentator utters the traditional 'They're off!'

And a strange thing happens: instead of the usual almighty mixture of sigh and roar, there is only a ragged murmur – it is as if we were about to witness not a contest but an exhibition.

And the commentator's voice is unfretted by excitement: it is as if he is reading from a prepared script.

From out vantage point, they seem to be racing on the rim of a great saucer.

The pace looks easy. And the field seems small because the eighteen runners are closely grouped.

When the field loosens a little, the blue of Riberetto leads the way. The red and yellow of Silver Season is just behind. Next comes Shergar's green.

And as they come down to Tattenham bend, the commentator's voice is clear above the barely murmuring crowd.

And there is a sense of inevitability as Shergar lopes to the front in the straight.

But suddenly the race seems to come alive as the tannoy tells that Lester Piggott is moving up smoothly on Shogun.

A great roar erupts – but the commentator has exaggerated.

The badger's blaze is coming smoothly nearer. The crowd are now quiet, resigned to the obvious.

About two hundred yards from home, young Walter Swinburn gives a quick peep behind him – and then pats his partner on the neck.

It is a remarkable gesture – almost as if a man fleeing from a bull had stopped to pick up a flower.

And he eases up as they come to the line – as if he feared that Shergar might overshoot the runway.

Glint of Gold and Scintillating Air come labouring in his wake. The rest of the field struggle in as scattered as the surviving Indians galloping away in the last reel.

And as Joe Mercer goes by on Sheer Grit, you realise that he is fifty and has ridden in umpteen Derbys and failed to win – and that Shergar's baby-faced pilot is only nineteen and has picked the golden apple at his first attempt.

Soon it is time to go back to Epsom, the township that has all the heady atmosphere of a suburban chemist's shop.

Its biggest pub, the Marquis of Granby, proclaims: 'Closed Tonight – Sorry'.

The visitor from another planet would think that the licentious soldiery were approaching.

The journey back through leafy south-west London is uneventful.

There is little talk of the race: Shergar has left no room for controversy.

But there is a moment that in retrospect seems like something experienced in a dream.

Neatly written up on the garage wall of a semi-detached in Wimbledon is: 'Up the Gorbals and Glasgow Celtic'.

It is like finding black puddings on the menu for the Royal wedding feast.

At Waterloo the disembarking pilgrims have to push

their way through commuters impatient to get on board.

And those sober-suited pillars of society look at us as the people of Epsom look on the gypsies.

Happily unconscious of all this, a pigeon sleeps in a quiet corner, squatting on the warm asphalt with wings outspread as if hatching imaginary eggs.

Monday night's rainstorm has left a great breast of water in the Thames.

Back in the Kings and Keys, the pub that justifies Fleet Street, mine host Andy gives his verdict.

'When you look back at it now,' he says, 'Shergar was a great price at evens.' And so he was.

On the plane back to Dublin I am luckier: I have a window seat – and can look down in awe at the gravel pits of Staines.

And next to me sits a brilliant man who has worked all over the world and is at the top of his profession – but doesn't make a song about it.

He is just in from Zurich – and hungry for a ringside account of the big race.

There is little to tell – and yet it is an exciting story.

And so over a few glasses of wine I try to express Shergar's impact.

One thinks of him as almost a different species from his rivals – as Muhammad Ali looked at his peak and as Pele did that day in Mexico City when Brazil swamped Italy in the final of the World Cup.

The two hundred and second Derby may not have been thrilling in the ordinary sense – but there is a great thrill in beholding greatness.

Evening Press, June 1981

Winter School

About twenty-five minutes and seventeen seconds past two of the clock on Wednesday the twenty-sixth of July I was accosted by one of my few remaining friends and he said, 'In the name of God, what's after happening you?'

This encounter – in case you'd like to know – took place in the afternoon rather than in the small hours; the place was Merrion Row in the city of Dublin.

We adjourned to O'Donoghue's and there I spun a tale: I was, I pretended, still suffering from the fallout engendered by the Munster final.

I doubted if he would believe the truth; about an hour previously, I had read an article on Dublin by an English journalist which didn't mention Mulligan's, the Long Hall or the Brazen Head.

Otherwise it was par for the course: there was the usual guff about the great conversation in the pubs, the proliferation of dark-eyed colleens and the excellence of a named brown stout.

And of course there was a great passage about certain writers and artists who have given rise to the cliché: 'There are no characters left.'

I was acquainted in varying degrees with most of those alleged characters – and, believe me, they were people whom you wouldn't take home to your granny, or even to your great-granny.

If a character is someone who 'borrows' money from you and then proceeds to bore the trousers off you, they are not scarce in the the Republic's capital.

And of course in that aforementioned article there was the statutory homage to James Joyce.

The old artificer has no greater admirer than I – but there is a difference between admiration and adulation.

I despise those people – and they are not thin on the ground – who deem every word he wrote as sacred.

In my not-so-humble opinion our Jim's reputation must rest on *Dubliners* and the *Portrait*.

To condemn *Ulysses* is about as foolhardy as casting aspersions on the Book of Kells or the Dingle dolphin or Sean Kinsella's cooking or the Artane Boys' Band – but I must confess that the alleged Great Irish Novel never moved me.

I have long felt it contains too much head and too little heart; at least to me, *Sons and Lovers* makes it look like a tediously contrived concoction.

And to deem it an accurate reproduction of Dublin on a certain day is rather naive: our Jim didn't even get the winner of the Gold Cup right.

Ulysses is, however, a mansend to thesis-hunters; sometimes I wonder whether our scholarly neighbours across the Atlantic would survive without it.

Doctorates have been spawned by studies of merely sections of it.

I have seen essays devoted to single paragraphs of it – and I find this incredibly funny: it is hardly a secret that *Ulysses* is riddled with misprints.

There is a Joyce Summer School at large in Dublin these

days; I wonder will anyone stand up and utter even a tiny criticism of the old artificer.

Now I see that the Abbey are about to stage all of W. B. Yeats's plays: God between us and all harm.

Ould Willie knew as much about drama as I do about aerobics. Let it pass: there is no arguing against fashion.

And that brings us to more serious matters, including the general attitude towards my native county.

I am not referring to the myth that every Kerry person is a born footballer. That subject is at present too painful; my complaint is rooted elsewhere.

I love the Dingle peninsula and I have spent many a happy day in the Barony of Iveragh but I wish those who write about travel and tourism would realise that there are other regions to explore in the Kingdom.

The term 'Ring of Kerry' symbolises the general attitude: it isn't the ring of Kerry, it is the ring of South Kerry.

One day some travel writer will discover the great moorland that extends north from a few miles above Castle Island to near Listowel – and west from Knocknagoshel to within a few miles of the Atlantic.

John B. Keane will tell you how much it influenced him. Of course it did: he can hardly write an article without mentioning Renagown or Lyrecrompane.

I have never seen it mentioned in any of those guides issued by the various tourist bodies.

All these worthy people seem fixed in their views: according to them, the real Ireland is along by the coast, preferably in the west.

Believe me, the inland parts of the country are real too, sometimes alarmingly so.

If you happen to be in West Munster, you might do worse than venture into the great moorland.

It is a lonely world in Winter but in early April it comes alive.

Then the pink-and-white of the flowering currant begins to decorate the hedges; work commences on the bog; the larks rise up out of the heather and sing for the sheer heaven of it.

Many people seem to look on sunbathing on some Mediterranean beach as the ideal holiday; count me out.

I have never taken a holiday – and I can imagine no better recreation than a fine day in the bog.

It is no place for the dilettante, but if you fall in love with it – as I did at first sight – you will quickly learn the relevant skills.

And when you pour the remains of the tea over the embers as you prepare to go home in the evening, you will experience a moment of especial loneliness.

The moorland breeds a hardy people but very few go in for Gaelic Football or any Football: they just couldn't afford to break a bone in the days between early April and October.

Eddie Walsh, the great Kerry wing-half-back, came from the moorland, but he was a special case. He worked as a timekeeper with the county council – and it didn't matter much if he broke a bone, even one of his own.

Jerry Kiernan, the celebrated long-distance runner, grew up in Brosna, on the eastern verge of that great expanse of bog and little fields.

And John Lenihan, great but more or less unsung, is another man whose matrix was the moorland.

John lives in Bearnageeha, the Windy Gap. He belongs to the parish of Ballymacelligot but has always been deemed a Castle Island man.

We have excellent grounds for claiming him: Ballymacelligott is a huge parish but doesn't contain a town or even a village. For the Lenihan family, the Island has always been their place for selling and buying.

And John runs for An Riocht, the club that fights out of my home town.

Now I will tell you a strange little story. Two Sundays ago, John competed in an exceptionally prestigious race; on Monday morning I searched the Irish papers for the result – in vain.

And so I was especially delighted when I saw my neighbour's name in a headline in the *Daily Telegraph*.

The event was the celebrated Snowdon Race at Llanberis in North Wales; if you labelled it the hill-runners' European championship, you wouldn't be far out.

The course is about five miles up and the same distance down. The field of over eight hundred included the famous Swiss runner, Martin May, and the English star, Malcolm Patterson.

John was second in his only other run in this race; that was three years ago.

This time he finished three hundred yards ahead of Patterson; May came in third.

It was a wonderful performance from a full-time farmer. It should have made the front pages here on the Monday; amazingly, it didn't make any pages at all.

John turned out for Sligo's Warriors' Race up and down Knocknarea last Friday evening – and galloped away with it.

A few years ago he led for much of the way in the Dublin City Marathon – but even John's mighty heart couldn't fight off the cramp that assailed him a few miles from the finishing line.

Anyhow, he, Jerry Kiernan and John Griffin have shown the world that there is more to Kerry than Football and fishing and 'traditional' music and ancient storytellers and mad *bodhrán*-makers and luscious black puddings and dark-eyed colleens wishing you the top of the evening.

Evening Press, 28 July 1989

THE BIG GAME
WHEN PRESSURE MEANT STEAM

The unknown aphorist who first said that it is better to travel hopefully than to arrive never experienced the joys of a thirty-six-hour flight from Gatwick to Auckland.

Nor was he ever on a wartime train from Kerry to Dublin. It was an endurance test at the best of times, and especially so on the way to an All-Ireland final: then the sheer weight of numbers slowed progress and even caused fears that the train wouldn't arrive in time.

There was no tannoy on the trains in those far-off days, and whenever the not-so-sweet chariot stopped for no obvious reason, panic would begin to raise its silly head.

And aficionados – they existed before Ernest Hemingway popularised the word – would begin to worry about having to 'watch' the match on the wireless in some pub in Tipperary perhaps or in Laois or maybe in Kildare itself.

It never happened, but in quite recent times a Derby special from Tralee failed to reach the Curragh in time for the big race. Some people were rather angry.

The preparations for those wartime journeys were in proportion to the expectations of delay.

To me they will forever be associated with the smell of freshly-cut ham; it was as much part of the big games as incense is of Benediction. And in my mind's eye I will forever see a sight that has now all but disappeared.

I see little groups of men walking steadily towards Croke Park becapped and solidly shod, topcoat slung over one shoulder and a big brown-paper-covered parcel firmly clutched.

They were the grass roots of the GAA – men who lived in a world where such words as 'motivation' and 'commitment' were unknown.

The word 'pressure' was at large but referred mainly to steam engines.

Now the comments before big games – in all codes – are littered with those three words.

You hear of players being not only under pressure, but under extra pressure.

And, of course, the accursed media are blamed by some people for unseemly incidents on and off the pitch.

It is forgotten by the media-bashers that not all wartime big games were graceful affairs; indeed the Football All-Ireland final of 1943 could charitably be described as a thundering disgrace.

The media barely existed then: there was no television, wireless sets were few, and the national papers consisted of only a few sheets.

And yet the hitman went about his nefarious trade.

For far too long the GAA have been very reluctant to concede that not all those who play its games are exemplary sportsmen.

There is, for example, no penalty-points system as in Soccer; in the GAA's scheme of things a player could be booked every Sunday and avoid suspension.

And, of course, the managerial revolution has exacerbated matters.

Occasionally you hear a manager say that he wouldn't have a hitman on his team; perhaps there are a few who are as good as their word.

I fear, however, that the majority have such a lust to win that their consciences become rather flexible in the context of sport.

Let us speak of better things. Since I made the hegira to Dublin, I miss a few aspects of rural life.

The fishing is one. I am a member of a Dublin club, but its rules restrict you to two trout per day.

I am afraid that I'm not yet ready for such a rigid regime.

And I miss 'coming up for the match'.

I have pleasant memories of making little fires on the Curragh and boiling the water and frying the black puddings.

It wasn't only Napoleon Bonaparte who believed that an army marches on its stomach.

It must be admitted, however, that the homeward journey could be tiresome, especially if your warriors had gone under.

For most of us, the idea of spending Sunday night in Dublin was a non-starter; work beckoned – and beckoned rather sternly.

Of course, the temptation to stay could be almost overpowering, but you would feel very guilty if you broke the peasant code.

I have a special memory of the night after Dublin had beaten Galway in the All-Ireland final of 1963.

I was in O'Donoghue's, not then as famous as it is now, but nevertheless a lively establishment.

I was in fair company: it included Sean Ó Murchú, Seamus Ennis, Ted Furey (yes, the dad), Aindreas Ó

Gallchoir and my travelling companions, the two Riordan brothers from Scartaglen.

Of course, all three of us would love to have stayed but, of course, we didn't.

The two lads had to be back at McElligott's garage in the morning; I had promised to take a few cattle to the fair with a neighbour.

The same neighbour's fences were not in the best of repair – and rounding up his bullocks in the dark of the pre-morning was not a congenial task for someone who wasn't in the best of repair himself.

On that Monday long ago I was – as they used to say in the country – 'hanging on by a thread'.

I had almost forgotten that phrase until a few days ago: it surfaced in a delightful letter from Ian Lee, a scholarly man who runs his godly race in Collins Lane, Tullamore – the capital of a county which I love.

Ian was sunning himself on the beach at Curracloe in deepest south-east Wexford when a back page of this paper drifted his way.

It included my oul' column; it was a piece mainly about the cutting of turf.

Ian writes that, although the taste of the sea was in his mouth, he could instantly smell the bog.

'I could see bog cotton, hear the squelch of bare feet – and taste my mother's egg sandwiches.'

Ian goes on: 'Many's the time I made the daily stroll to the well with a gallon can brought from a good old-fashioned tinker . . . '

And that day below in Curracloe a certain occasion came back to him with especial vividness.

'My neighbours – some of them long since gone – were there.

'Jack Hannify was on the slean – and not in the best of shape.

'My father – gladly still fit and able to go to the bog – was fixing poor Jack with a look not a bit sympathetic and urging him to throw out the last few precious sods before the water rushed in, the dam broke or the whole bog caved in.'

Ian says, 'In those far-off days, I didn't understand the effects a night drinking porter in Finlay's of Mount Bolus had on a turf-cutting performance.'

And how did Jack Hannify reply to the urgings of Ian's da?

'Dear God, Lee, I'm hanging on by a thread.'

Evening Press, 16 August 1989

'WICKET' SEASON FOR ENGLAND

Estyn Evans, who departed this earthly world a few days ago, was as wise a man as ever came out of Wales – and that is saying a great deal.

I never met him but I read all his books and they immensely enriched me; he was a great geographer in the fullest sense of the word.

The geography that most of us acquired at school wasn't too bad; at least it gave us a fair idea of how the land and the water lie.

And we learned about the cotton towns of Lancashire and the wool towns of Yorkshire – and we discovered to our delight and astonishment that most of the needles used by our mothers and sisters were made in a little town called Redditch.

We didn't, however, learn much about our own country or our own townlands. We weren't encouraged to look around us and ask, for example, why some hedges were straight lines and others so crooked that they seemed to have been plotted by a madman.

Estyn Evans followed what is known as the French humanist concept of geography – at least as much as a Welshman can follow anything.

This essentially is about the relationship between man and his environment – and of course it embraces what we have come to know as history. The truth is that history and geography are one.

History, as most of us learned it, is mainly concerned with politics, with broad movements that visibly bring about change; of day-to-day life we found out little.

Estyn Evans spent most of his working life in Belfast and of course was acutely aware of its tribal tensions; in hardly any other part of the world was there a greater need to dispel myth and establish truth.

The island is woefully bedevilled by myths; what is – wrongly, perhaps – labelled the Christian Brothers' concept of history is about as veracious as the popular image of how the West was won.

The glorification of the Gael was akin to the Nazis' theory of Aryan superiority, but it must be admitted that not all its consequences were sinister: some were rather hilarious.

I am thinking especially of the infamous Ban promulgated by the Gaelic Athletic Association; lads and lassies of this generation must find its ramifications almost incredible.

It is a topic of which I am tired; I am glad that I have lived to see the day when playing a 'foreign' game doesn't have you branded as an inferior Irishman.

Incidentally, I was saddened when I heard a few days ago that an Antrim Hurling club had its goalposts cut down. That's the other side of the coin.

Not all the news is bad: Cricket has been revived in my own county, probably because some enthusiasts from the subcontinent of India are working down there.

A club has sprung up in Tralee; they have played a series of matches; as yet, no angry Celtic or Gaelic god has hurled a thunderbolt at the miscreants.

The ignorant who, it seems, will be always with us, look

on this ancient game as a preserve of the upper classes. It is far from it; indeed there was an era when it was banned in England because men with damaged hands were less efficient as labourers and archers.

And for long it has been as much the game of the English coalminers as Rugby is of their Welsh fellows.

And in the last century and for part of this it was popular in many parts of Ireland, as students of Canon Sheehan and Francis Ledwidge know.

Then came the green deluge: all things deemed foreign were suspect. The lunacy reached its pinnacle one day in Leitrim when a big march was organised to protest against 'jazz'. You don't believe it? It happened.

Cricket is a marvellous game, not least because it provides for all kinds of physical types and because you needn't put away your bat as you approach the two score.

And not the least of its appeal is its tactical depth: it makes all other field games look exceedingly simple.

A captain in Cricket is rather more than someone who partakes in the toss, decides who takes the place-kicks, and offers the odd few words' encouragement. When his team are fielding, he must be as acutely aware as a hen minding chickens in a land where hawks abound.

By moving a fielder as little as a few yards, he can transform the shape of a match; the tactical subtleties are infinite.

So is the variety of deliveries available to the bowlers: that department has a fascinating vocabulary.

'Chinaman', 'yorker' and 'googly' are fairly familiar, but not everybody knows what a 'bosey' is. It is an exaggerated form of the googly: it was called after a professional cricketer named Bosanquet. You may remember one of his sons: he had a rather colourful career as a newsreader on television.

Quick bowling is dramatic – sometimes melodramatic – but the various kinds of spin are to Cricket as caviare is to cuisine.

Those of us who are older remember two modest little men from the West Indies who so bewitched England a generation ago; in the process they helped their team win a series in the game's home for the first time.

They were duly immortalised in a lovely calypso. It begins, 'Cricket, lovely Cricket, at Lord's where they play it', and the chorus goes:

> *With those two little pals of mine,*
> *Ramadhin and Valentine.*

In the meantime, the men from the West Indies have relied mainly on pace. Suddenly a crop of giants seems to have sprung up amongst them: Ramadhin and Valentine appear to have come from a different world.

Once upon a time the term 'six-footer' conveyed that a man was exceptionally tall; if you happen to be in O'Connell Street at rush hour nowadays, you will see that six-footers are almost as common as daisies in a May field.

And the emergence of bowlers who are well over six feet has been a boon to makers of headgear and has prompted some gurus to suggest that the distance between the wickets should be increased.

That is unlikely to happen: it would make life too difficult for those men who depend on guile rather than pace.

Evening Press, 25 August 1989

The Golden Age of the Train

It was the day after Pope John had gone into the good night. The five women who boarded the train at Rathmore spoke of hardly anything else until we came to Headford Junction.

There a gang of men were taking up the line that led to Kenmare. One of the women said: 'When you think of all the work that went into putting down that line, you wonder what is the sense in taking it up.'

Her companions agreed and I nodded my head. I was glad to get into the conversation and I told them that Pope John had been a man like ourselves, the son of a small farmer in the village of Sotte del Monte.

I said that he too would have been sad to see that rail link being taken up. He was a peasant and had a sound sense of values. My travelling companions too were peasants in the purest sense of the word.

It was about twelve o'clock on a Saturday. They had voluminous shopping bags. Of course they were going on an expedition to Killarney. They wouldn't buy anything that couldn't be had in Rathmore.

It was a day out. They would have tea and cakes in some café and come home that evening with all the news from the big town. My mother would have been at home with them. They spoke the same language.

They loved the railway. To travel by road was making a journey; on the train you embark on an adventure. My mother used to go to Tralee with the excuse of paying the rates, something that could have been done in Castle Island on a Fair Day.

It was bad enough to close down the rail links; it was criminal to dig up the track. A lovely horizontal ladder gave way to a weed-filled scar. It was ugly and uneconomical.

Very few people shouted 'Stop'. Myles na gCopaleen campaigned for years in the *Irish Times* against this madness. I did my modest bit in the *Kerryman* and in the *Evening Press*.

We were like mice speaking in a wood in a thunderstorm. The madness went on. The economists had all the answers. If a rail link didn't pay, it went the way of all steel and wood.

I had long believed that most economists know all the answers but haven't heard all the questions. They excel in explaining why something happened but not why they hadn't foreseen it.

Nobody ever argues that a section of a road doesn't pay – but if a gang came and started to dig it up, there would be an outcry and worse.

Some things cannot be measured by numbers. At home in Kerry we lived about three hundred feet above the valley; my mother loved to see the trains coming and going down below. They were a symbol of energy.

The trains were like rivers. They were a kind of poetry. They were much more than that: they carried a good deal of merchandise and left the roads comparatively free for passenger traffic.

It isn't yet too late to repair the damage but the wanton destruction of the link lines will make the task all the more costly.

If you ever see a map of our rail network in its prime, you will understand why it was the envy of the rest of Europe – it penetrated into every nook and cranny in the island.

There is a copy under the counter in Charlie St George's pub in Limerick; that famous tavern is just across the road from the railway station. Whenever that map is unrolled for me, I look back in anger and in sadness.

The women in the train between Rathmore and Killarney on that Saturday long ago got it right. It was a pity that some public-opinion analyst wasn't around at the time. The vote would have been overwhelmingly in favour of keeping the railways.

The train was the people's friend. When my mother went to Tralee, the return journey cost little. There is now no public transport between our town and Kerry's capital. If you haven't a car, you have to hire a hackney.

I need hardly add that there is a sense of romance about travelling by train. I know the streets between Burgh Quay and Lansdowne Road fairly well but whenever I travel by train, I seem to be in a new and wondrous country.

I suspect that many of my neighbours at home long ago had a kindred feeling: Tralee is only ten miles from our town by road; it is fifteen by rail, but on the day of a Football game they loved to go by train.

There was method in their sanity: most of them would otherwise have gone by bike – and they believed that if you drink a fair amount, you shouldn't cycle. Thus they had no worry about coming home. The train wouldn't stop at any halfway house.

When they got back home safely – as most of them

did – they spoke of their adventures as if they had been on the *Orient Express*. It was an age of marvellous innocence.

There are so many stories about the railway and the train that they would make a nice book, and it wouldn't be a slim volume. I will be content to tell just one.

The hero was a man called Maurice Keane. He lived in a bog about a mile from our town. He wasn't over-burdened with education but he was famous for his sense of humour and his wit.

A time came when he had to go to Dublin. It was so long ago that what is now Portlaoise was then known as Maryboro.

He positioned himself at the ticket window. He was the last in a queue of four. He decided to take his cue from the girl in front of him. She said, 'Maryboro. Third. Single.' He said, 'Maurice Keane. Fourth. Married.'

THE HUMBLE SPUD

They are little poems in themselves: the Arran Banner, the Dunbar Rover, the May Queen, the Kerr's Pink, the Golden Wonder, the British Queen, the Epicure and the Champion, not to mention the Record and the Sharpe's Express.

Count in the Rooster – the latest addition to the kingdom of the potato – and many others that have names that are embedded in peasant folklore.

I wonder did Walter Raleigh foresee the economic revolution that he set in motion when he brought a handful of tubers to Ireland from the New World.

I grew up in an age when the potato was to us as the rice is to the good people of Eastern Asia. It was a special delight to us small boys: we hadn't yet encountered the word 'barbecue', but we had our own version. We loved to make a fire in the open and roast potatoes over it.

Of course there was a greater treat: the potatoes left over after the dinner were roasted on the embers before bedtime. With butter and a pinch of salt, you had a repast too good for most kings. It was even better if you had buttermilk.

Not the least of the potato's attractions was that you could cook it in several ways. You could boil it or roast or bake it or serve it as chips.

Alas, the potato is all too often served up as chips without being parboiled. This is sacrilege – there should be a law against it.

In the course of a rather varied career, I was once deemed an expert in cutting seed. That was funny, because it is a simple trade. There was no experience needed – it was only a matter of taking care.

The first rule was that you should never let a faulty *scilleán* get past you – a *scilleán* was a potato seed.

The slightest sign of black was a warning. Such flawed seeds were put aside and boiled for the fowl and the pigs. The next rule concerned the number of sprouts – or eyes, as they were called.

If a potato had only one eye, you despatched it to the boiling pot. Most potatoes have several; the rule was to have at least two and not more than three in your *scilleán*.

You could get two *scilleáns* out of most potatoes. If there was a piece left over, it went to the pot. Seed-cutting time was good for the fowl and the pigs.

One night long ago, as I watched a film about the occupation of France during World War Two, I encountered a homely scene.

A young girl who was a member of the Resistance was in hiding in a remote farmhouse; it is Spring and she is helping with the cutting of the seed. The old woman of the house advises her: 'Not less than two or more than three.'

Why should you cut the potato so that the *scilleán* hasn't more than three eyes? Too many sprouts would weaken the *scilleán* – you would have too much foliage.

Whenever I finished cutting a lot of seed, I gave the *scilleáns* a good dusting of lime. This was to discourage the slugs and the snails and the wireworms.

There was another rule in the peasant's catalogue: have

the *scilleáns* in the ground before Saint Patrick's Day. The early potatoes were, of course, already in the earth – usually by mid-February.

There is a great thrill in seeing the first shoots peer above the ground. In a normal year – if we ever have such in Ireland – your early potatoes should be ready for eating in late June. The first meal of them was a special occasion in rural Ireland.

It evoked a familiar prayer: 'May we all be alive again this time next year.'

The frost is the great enemy of the early potato. It can reduce a lovely green garden to a horrible, dark-brown mess.

The elders in my youth had two ways of counteracting the frost. One way was to light a fire at night in the corner of the garden whence the wind came. It wasn't very effective. Neither was the other plan – pulling a sack along the stalks before the sun rose.

In a rare rush of intelligence, I thought of a foolproof plan. Give shelter to your stalks by planting curly kale alongside them – it is impregnable to frost. Leeks can serve this purpose too but kale is better.

I will give you another hint: put down Kerr's Pinks in February and they are as good as any early variety.

There was intense rivalry among our neighbours long ago about who would have the early potatoes ready for the table first. You couldn't believe everybody in this context: I used to take around gifts of the precious tubers to our closest friends as proof.

I must confess that it was more out of vanity than generosity.

You can enjoy the Kerr's Pink in June but it isn't until

September that you find it at its glorious best. That is the time for making potato cakes; the mixture of flour and potatoes is called farina – a lovely word.

The main-crop potatoes are usually harvested in October. This is the hens' harvest too. Whenever they see you going towards the garden with a spade, they need no invitation.

They love the fat worms that you find in potato ground. As his flock enjoys the harvest, the cock is nonplussed – there is no need for him to dig. He is like a minister without portfolio.

Some people are too proud, incidentally, to make potato cakes – they deem it a mark of poverty. Thus the potato has its place in social snobbery.

The West Kerry Gaeltacht is not free from this ailment. They have a saying there: 'We never had to eat the spuds for our breakfast.' I did, and still do – you couldn't make a better start to the day.

The Champion, alas, is extinct. It was a beautiful potato – white, with a red band and a deep hollow in its base. Seemingly it became too vulnerable to blight.

The spud was the ingredient of many a traditional dish. Colcannon was an example. This was potato mashed with shredded cabbage – the mixture was crowned with butter.

This dish is celebrated in a well-known song. The chorus goes like this:

> Oh she did, oh she did,
> She did and so did I.
> And the more I think about it,
> It nearly makes me cry.

Weren't they the happy days
When troubles we had not,
And our mothers made colcannon
In the little skillet pot.

Patrick Kavanagh of course paid his homage to the noble spud. 'The flocks of green potato stalks were blossoms spread for sudden flight. The Kerr's Pinks in a frivelled blue. The Arran Banner wearing white.'

Walter Raleigh, alas, did not live happily ever after.

He was a man of great ability and infinite courage. But he became too powerful for his own good.

His enemies at the court laid false information about him and he was stripped of his high offices and imprisoned in the Tower of London. He was beheaded in the Autumn of 1618.

It was a sad end for the man who brought us the potato.

What's in a Name?

I have a friend who always pronounces Dún Laoghaire and Portlaoise and other Gaelic place names as they are spelled. Some people might think that this is pretentious. I don't; indeed, I love this respect for language.

Place names are part of our heritage: they are a kind of people's poetry. I get terribly irritated when, for example, someone pronounces Rathmore as it is written.

It is a great pity that so many of our place names have become Anglicised and thus corrupted. Ballyhooly is an example; originally it was Béal Atha na hUlla, 'the mouth of the apple ford'.

I have been interested in place names since I was a child. When I couldn't work out the meaning of a place name, it irked like a pebble under my mind's door. My excuse for this failure to crack their code is that they are pre-Celtic.

There are some place names in my part of Kerry that baffle even scholars; it is a wry consolation. I have another source of consolation: the scholars aren't always right. Sometimes they are wildly off the mark.

Not too long ago there was a regular feature on Radio Éireann about place names. The experts were men and women renowned for their scholarship; like many scholars, they lacked common sense.

One night they set about explaining Lyrecompane to a grateful public. I listened with bated breath – whatever that means. As those intrepid people went on and on, I delighted at their lack of understanding. And their collective confidence produced a ludicrous explanation.

All this illustrated a belief of mine: when you meet a difficult name such as Lyrecompane, you must see the place. Lyrecompane means 'the horseshoe of land under the cliff'.

The River Smearla encloses a horseshoe of land under a cliff: when you see it, you understand. The word 'ladhar' basically means the amount of meal or flour or whatever that you can enclose by bringing your hands together. The experts in RTÉ didn't get it quite right.

A little to the east of my home town, Castle Island, you can find an interesting example of how names change. Two rivers meet there – or, to be accurate, a river and a stream.

The river is called Seanabha, which means, I suppose, 'the old river' or 'the big river'. The stream has two names: 'the Spring' and 'the Muing'.

Now here is the interesting aspect: when the two waters meet, their product takes the name of the lesser. And it goes boldly on its way towards the Atlantic as the Maine, an Anglicisation of Muing.

When a name changes, it isn't always corrupted, even if it loses some of its meaning. Gleannsharoon is an example. It is the name of a townland about two miles north-east of Castle Island.

We were told at school that it means 'Geoffrey's Glen', after Geoffrey de Marisco, who had built a castle there in the twelfth century. Even as a small boy, I wasn't convinced.

I am almost certain that the name means 'the valley of the bitter apples': Gleann na Searbh Ulla. For about three of its seven miles, the river that runs through the valley has crab-apple trees on both banks.

How do place names originate? You could ask the same question about language. Words do not originate from committees or brains trusts – they come from individuals.

The coiners of words are primal poets; if the word is apt, the tribe adopts it. Place names are a clue to the minds of a people. Some people possess a poetic imagination; others tend to be pragmatic. They use place names as a marker.

Knocknagoshel provides an interesting study as a place name. It seems to mean 'the hill of the castles', but I doubt if there was ever any castle there. There was a time when it was called Mountcashel. It also had another name: the Mall.

I have heard some of the older generations call it simply 'Mall' – 'I was over in the Mall last night.' This gave rise to a story that to me seems peculiarly Irish.

It goes back to the early twentieth century, when our part of Ireland was in the throes of a Westminster election. A billposter returned from his day's work and told his employer – that rare being, an innocent politician – how he had fared. 'I put up your bills in three villages today: Knocknagoshel, Mountcashel and the Mall,' he said.

Why has the village with three names become so much a part of our folklore? The story goes back to the Parnellite split. On a certain Sunday, the Chief was due to address a meeting in Newcastle West. His supporters in the mountain parish marched to the meeting behind a remarkable banner. It proclaimed a simple message: 'Arise Knocknagoshel and Take Your Place Among the Nations of the Earth'.

One of the most fascinating place names known to me is the label for a cluster of narrow streets in the very heart of London. Soho was once out in the country – it was marshland.

Men coursed hares there. 'So-ho, so-ho, so-ho,' is the sound you make when you are trying to catch a hare in its form. I have seen it done.

The name of London itself is a Celtic word. Long Dún means a safe place for ships. And so when next you are in London, you can feel at home there.

If you are in Piccadilly or Leicester Square or in the other Mall, you can say to yourself 'We christened this town.'

BIRDS OF A FEATHER

There is a modest field on the eastern side of the road from Castle Island to Dublin that should have a preservation order put on it – not because I spent so many hours working there, but because it is such a marvellous unofficial bird sanctuary.

A stream runs by the far side of the field: it is sheltered by a bank about eight feet high and is the birds' ideal watering place.

On the northern boundary of the field there are two cherry trees and a plum tree, all once of course having accompanied a dwelling but long since gone wild. On the other two boundaries there is an abundance of hawthorn and blackberry bushes. This is good nesting territory.

One of those boundaries separates the field from the road but the proximity to busy traffic doesn't inhibit birds from setting up house there.

In this field I acquired one invaluable lesson – do not look on experts as infallible. You will be told, for example, that birds sing to mark out their territory; they do, but there is more to it than that.

From my own humble observations, I discovered that birds often sing for the sheer joy of it. I discovered too that the term 'bird-brained' is woefully misguided. Birds are wonderfully resourceful; they can adapt to changing conditions as quickly as Kerry people in exile.

Sometimes I ask myself which is my favourite bird. The truth is that there are so many favourites that I have no favourite. The starling would be a prime candidate: he is a maligned bird.

People tend to think of him as unhandsome and raucous; at close quarters you will see his brilliantly spotted plumage – electric green and red and blue. The starling can sing but, alas, he has no songs of his own: he sings snatches of other birds' tunes.

My father's generation, incidentally, referred to the starling as 'the stare' – that, of course, was the original name. The starling is the ultimate socialist. They show this when the ground is frozen: you will see them foraging in flocks, but though food is scarce, they never fight over it.

They live in communities but this doesn't prevent essays in private enterprise. I have never seen a starling on its own but it is common to see two or three foraging together.

In Dublin in the early 1970s they provided a grand sight about an hour before dark every evening as they congregated on the television masts over Clery's and nearby buildings. These gatherings are now past-tense. The polluted air may be the cause.

Most of us grew up believing that the wren is our smallest bird. It isn't – that honour belongs to the goldcrest. Although goldcrests have become comparatively common since the proliferation of the forests, not everybody has seen one.

In the distance, you can mistake a goldcrest for a butterfly. If you are ever bait-fishing, as distinct from fly-fishing, by a tree-lined river, you have a good chance of seeing one. Because you are almost still, the little bird mistakes you for a tree and moves around freely.

The dipper is another bird not often seen, because it tends to frequent quiet stretches of water. It is about the same size as a blackbird; it is dark-brownish and has a white breast.

The dipper makes its living by standing on rocks over shallow water and fishing on the bed. It cannot swim but it walks on the bed of the river and depends mainly on micro-life.

Most people will agree that the kingfisher is our loveliest bird; we see him only in multicoloured electric flashes. High chalk banks are his favourite habitat; unlike the dipper, he has a powerful beak and lives on small fish.

In a previous incarnation, I was often on 'the wran' but we wouldn't dream of killing the little bird to take him as a trophy. We loved the tiny bird for his darting ways and his amazing capacity for survival.

Because there is a strain of roguery in most of us, we admired him all the more for the story about the birds' World Cup final, even though it is only a fable.

My generation all know the story – it was in the school books in our primary days. The birds all came together to see who could fly the highest.

After a long Midsummer Day, the eagle emerged as victor. He spread his wings wide and said, 'I am the king.' Little did he know: the wren flew out of his plumage – and the stowaway said, 'No, I am the king.'

In the aftermath of the All-Ireland Football final in 1982, you could hardly blame some of Kerry's supporters if they suspected that Seamus Darby was a wren in a previous incarnation.

In Dublin's fair city, I miss the abundant bird life of the country. We have, of course, those citizens of the world – the sparrows and the pigeons. On the canals and the rivers we have the mallard and the water hens and the swans.

Then there is the resident cormorant that plies his trade between Liberty Hall and the Clarence Hotel. One day about five years ago I watched him in a bizarre drama.

Five small seagulls were dive-bombing him – in vain. He submerged and came up a few yards upstream. This went on for about ten minutes; then the gulls gave up. You could see the cormorant laughing as he resumed his search for eels and small fish.

The scene was in the middle of the river off Burgh Quay, opposite the *Irish Press* building of fond and loving memory.

If you are lucky, you may see a heron going about his business. You have a good chance of seeing him downstream at the bridge over the Tolka in Drumcondra.

Few people are aware that the robin can sing: indeed he can, and sing marvellously. He is usually silent until about an hour before dark; then he sings with a remarkable fusion of power and sweetness.

What I miss most in Dublin is the Winter invasion of birds from Scandinavia and elsewhere in the north. In our part of Kerry the most common visitors are the fieldfare and the redwing thrush. I haven't forgotten the Summer immigrants – the swallow and cuckoo and the corncrake. We rarely hear the corncrake now because the meadows are cut much earlier to make silage. You will hear him now mainly in marshy land.

I heard a great story lately on *Mooney Goes Wild*. Two jackdaws came back and found that a pot had been placed over the chimney in which they had nested the year before. They failed to dislodge it but didn't give up. They went away and came back with about fifty of their comrades; the pot was soon demolished. We should be very slow to use the term 'birdbrain'.

I need hardly add that birds have their part in poetry and song. When it was expected that a French invasion would free Ireland, somebody wrote a ballad about Napoleon Bonaparte in which he is called 'the Green Linnet'.

Charles Stewart Parnell was, of course, 'the Blackbird of Avondale'. Who was 'the Kerry Eagle'? It wasn't Mick O'Connell or Jack O'Shea, or Maurice Fitzgerald. It was their neighbour Daniel O'Connell.

Ancient Learning

The scene was a pub in Fleet Street, before that wonderful heartland of journalism became a hive of yuppies. The barmaids were in a state of near-hysteria: a power cut had disrupted their world.

Pens and pencils and scraps of paper were rushed into service to determine the price of multiple orders. As a graduate of a different generation in primary education, I laughed uproariously to myself.

And I thought of the long but far from lost days when the morning half-hour in our national school was devoted to mental arithmetic. 'A dozen and a half eggs at a penny ha'penny an egg. Come on, come on.' 'How many inches in a yard and three quarters?'

'If it took three men two hours to dig a hole, how long would it take five men?' Thus the craic went on – with the occasional trap, such as: 'If it took ten minutes to boil an egg, how long would it take to boil three eggs?'

Our wits were honed in that noisy academy – you learned that the answer to an 'easy' question isn't always the obvious one. 'A hundred of cabbage plants at tuppence a plant.' The answer was tuppence multiplied by a hundred and ten – the number of plants in our hundred.

Primary education then may not have been as sophisticated as it is now, but it didn't lack merit. Those who were inclined to learn – or even only half-inclined – came away with a fair knowledge of English and Arithmetic.

We also had a smattering of Irish – but it was superficial because it hadn't been so much taught as inflicted. Of course we were introduced to History but the teaching was inclined to be rather chauvinistic.

Thus we went out into the world convinced that Ireland had beaten Denmark in the final of the World Cup on Good Friday in 1014.

Nobody told us that many Danes went back to their ships and enjoyed a hearty Scandinavian supper and went on dominating the commercial life of Leinster and beyond.

We learned geography, kind of . . . 'Name the principal towns of Roscommon.' 'Roscommon, Boyle and Elephant.' This was intended to drive the teacher mad.

We could sing out the cotton towns of Lancashire and the wool towns of Yorkshire. And we were thrilled to discover that the needles used by our mothers and sisters were all made in Redditch.

Of course we in Kerry were very proud that Carrauntoohil was the highest mountain in Ireland – you would think that we had built it ourselves. Of real geography, we were taught little: we didn't even known that milk was to our local economy as coal and iron were to South Wales.

And we didn't know how the fields and roads of our locality had evolved; we took it for granted that they were always there. It wasn't the fault of our teachers; they were people of their times.

'Environment' and 'ecology' weren't then in our vocabulary; today they are words of which we are becoming more and more aware. I think of what the good people of Iceland will tell you: 'Ours is an island surrounded by fish – take away the fish and there is no more Iceland.'

The good people of New Zealand have a similar outlook: 'We depend on our agriculture and our fishing. Pollute our land and our water and there is no more New Zealand.' All this recalls a famous dictum uttered by Saint Thomas Aquinas: 'The farmer doesn't own the land – he holds it in stewardship for the common good.'

We are all citizens of the global village that we call our home: it is the duty of every individual to leave it better than he found it. This was not stressed in our days in primary school; there was little or no awareness of the environment. Now, with heavy industrialisation in most parts of the world, this awareness is growing.

The need for clean energy is one of the biggest questions facing the new century. Fossil fuels have two obvious flaws: they are unlikely to last indefinitely, and they cause pollution.

The sun and the winds and the tides will be harnessed more and more – only vested interests and a lack of political will stand in the way. The disposal of waste is an immediate problem for us here in Ireland – and indeed in many parts of the world.

To bury or to burn, that is the question. A time will come when that problem will be irrelevant. The people of New Zealand believe that by 2020 they will have reduced their waste to zero. It is a heartening forecast and should encourage all of us who care about the environment.

We will see paper compressed into blocks for building. Sewage will no longer go into the sea – it will be transformed into energy. All this was far from our thoughts when we were in secondary school; the teaching of History and

Geography there was much the same as in the primary school.

History was mainly about battles and wars; the common people were invisible. Geography was mainly about topography: about countries and cities and towns and deserts and mountains and rivers and lakes.

We could all tell the height of Mount Everest but we hadn't a clue about the lives of the people who lived underneath it. One of our teachers was obsessed with the capitals of states and countries – and therein lies a tale.

On the wall we had a map of North America, with all of the United States clearly coloured. One day all of our class – about twenty of us – were looking up at that lovely map as we were put through our paces. 'O'Connor, take the pointer and show us the capital of New York.' 'Yes sir, Albany, sir.' 'Donovan, show us the capital of Massachusetts.' 'Yes sir, Boston, sir.'

Thus it went on with no problem until it came to the capital of Vermont. Several lads in turn shouted out 'Montpelier' but couldn't point it out – and were verbally lashed. Vermont is a very small state – and eventually the terrible truth dawned on the teacher: Montpelier wasn't on the map at all.

A teacher's lot isn't always a happy one.

The secondary school left us with one great heritage: we knew reams of English poetry. We didn't just memorise it, we knew it by heart. This came about because in the course of preparation for the Intermediate and the Leaving we repeated our poetry over and over; much of it stayed with us forever.

And in the bog and in the pub we often broke out in

verse: somebody would sing out a stanza, somebody else would follow, and so it went. The generation before us took great pride in the store of poetry that they knew by heart.

We had a neighbour who when he had a few drinks in him used to boast that he could recite the two best poems in the English language word for word. They were 'The Elegy, In a Country Churchyard' and 'The Deserted Village'. And he could, if you gave him his head. We used to stop him before he got too far by asking him to give us a song.

Now I will tell you a bizarre story. It concerns the book prescribed for the Leaving Certificate poetry about thirty years ago. Not surprisingly, the poems were numbered; there was nothing wrong with that.

Alas, however, some unsung genius in the Department of Education got a rush of blood to the head and decided that the even numbers should alternate with the odd numbers from year to year as the prescribed texts.

No doubt it seemed a splendid idea at the time and probably got promotion for its begetter. There was, however, a flaw. Some young people love poetry and of course read all the poems in the book, irrespective of the numbers. In the examination, it was stressed that quotations should come from prescribed poems.

Thus the young person who loved poetry not wisely but too well might quote from the 'wrong' poems. There was another flaw, less obvious but more far-reaching. A man who had done his Leaving in the even years might find himself married to a girl from the odd years.

Think about it – this could lead to a grevious hollow in communications.

THE GLORY THAT WAS WALES

If you asked me to name mankind's greatest curse, I wouldn't hesitate. I would like to bury nationalism at a crossroads and drive a stake through its heart. Now read on . . .

The Republic of Ireland Soccer team have no more fervent follower than me. And if you are ever near me when Kerry are in action, you may hear wild and whirling words.

The nationalism that I detest is essentially negative: it has as much to do with hating some other country as loving your own. At a very early age, I began to distrust this brand of nationalism.

My father, God rest him, was the cause of my new awareness – even if more or less unwittingly. In his youth he had worked in the Welsh coalfield, not as a miner but as a fitter's apprentice in the pits. He learned to love the miners – and the Welsh people in general.

Indeed, in later years when games of Rugby between our countries were broadcast, I sometimes suspected that his loyalty was divided. Anyhow, from listening to him, I began to believe that the Irish were not the only great people in the world.

And as I inevitably grew older and learned more about the make-up of Irish society, I formed a statement to express my view of the world. It is this: 'The Welsh miner is my brother; the Irish gombeen man is my enemy.'

Even if that same gombeen man had a rake of All-Ireland

medals, he would still be my enemy. Alas, the Welsh miner is no more; the Irish gombeen man is proliferating.

My father worked in two Welsh towns, Ebbw Vale and Mountain Ash. A few years ago, I found myself within striking distance of Ebbw Vale and decided to pay my respects.

I had the excuse of going to watch Ebbw Vale playing London Irish in the Anglo-Welsh Cup. So two of us drove up from Cardiff into the heart of the mountains. Believe it or not, the signposting in Wales is worse than in Ireland.

After much enquiring and the occasional turn back, we reached the sacred place. And I said to my father, then long departed this mortal world, 'I am here.'

I wasn't disappointed: the people were friendly in the only pub we visited and they spoke the language, kind of . . .

Incidentally, if you ever decide to visit mid-Wales in Winter, prepare yourself as if for a polar expedition. The people may be warm, but their habitat is cold, very cold.

Mountain Ash is still awaiting the privilege of our visit. Since first I set foot in Wales, many a flood has gone under the bridge, and a few over the bridges – the Dodder did it a few years ago.

I have told the story before in a book called *Windfalls* – allow me to tell some of it again.

I voyaged in the old MV *Inisfallen*, of fond memory. We set out from Penrose Quay in the heart of Cork about half past six in the evening. About one o'clock in the non-human hours, I got my first glimpse of Wales.

I spied a very faint glimmer of light to the east. It grew almost imperceptibly as we sailed onwards.

It was the loneliest sight that I ever saw: it was a help to know from the map that it came from the lighthouse on Strumble Head.

When we docked, I heard a soft lilting voice in the darkness: 'Take her to Goodwick, Dai.' I knew that I was in a foreign land. Dai, incidentally, was the driver of a locomotive; Goodwick is a village in Fishguard Bay.

In the meantime, I have come to know Wales fairly well. It is a lovely country and it has lovely people. The old language is alive and well in parts of the mountain country and parts of the west.

I first heard it spoken early one morning in a London hotel – it was the news on the radio. I understood only the occasional word but I loved the sound of it.

I bought a Welsh dictionary – not to help learn the language but to understand the place names. Place names are a key to a people's way of seeing the world.

Some people see poetically – with their imagination. Some see pragmatically – with what they deem common sense.

The Welsh have as much common sense as any people – they need it to survive in a harsh environment – but their place names are often poetic.

Once upon a time I played Rugby against a team called Tonyrafeil. I was delighted to learn the meaning of the name: 'the sound of the anvil'.

On that morning long ago when first I sampled Wales, I was on the way to London, the Kerryman's home from home. For the first hour or so, we travelled through farmland: this is where the old language is at its strongest.

Soon we were into South Wales; coal and iron were still king. For a young man from rural Ireland, this was a new world. It was still only about three o'clock, but the symphony of lights was marvellous to behold.

There was the glow from the steel mills and the blast furnaces – and the lights of the cars coming down from the valleys.

I had left home about seven the previous day but suddenly the tiredness left me: energy creates energy. Industrial Wales is now only a memory; the great docks of Cardiff are only a museum.

The Welsh are a resilient people; for generations, they have known that whether it is wintertime or summertime, the living is never easy. It is no coincidence that the leek is their national emblem: that plant will grow almost anywhere.

Parts of Wales went through very bad times in the 1930s, the era of 'love on the dole'. Laver bread became part of the diet; it was made from flour and seaweed. It was hardly a delicacy.

In bad times you will find that sport becomes very important. We tend to think that Rugby is the only sporting passion in Wales, but it has a great tradition in Boxing too.

Believe it or not, there are parts of Wales where Rugby is second to Soccer. If you are ever at a game in Anfield, cathedral of Liverpool FC, you will realise this. You will see coaches from many parts of North Wales – coaches with wheels.

Music is, of course, the greatest of Welsh passions. One night long ago on the boat from Fishguard to Rosslare, a young Welshman confessed to me: 'My ambition is to conduct Handel's *Oratorio* and to captain Wales to the Triple Crown.'

Poetry is of course music's sister. Wales, like Ireland, has a huge body of poetry in the old language. For good measure, it can boast of two leading modern poets in the English language.

R. S. Thomas is that rare poet – he has written in both Welsh and English. He is a counterpart of my friend, Michael Hartnett, who has written in English and in Gaelic.

Dylan Thomas is the most famous poet in modern English. He was a monster; you wouldn't take him home to your mother, even if you were certain that she was out. He was a thief and a sponger and a cheat – but he was a magician with words.

He is one of my icons: I often go back to his work for refreshment. He was thirty-nine when he died in a New York hospital. It was a Saturday evening. His last coherent words were poetry in themselves: 'Tonight at home the men are in the pubs – and they have their arms around each other and they are singing.'

Thomas grew up in Swansea; he grew up even more in the Welsh countryside. There as a boy he spent holidays with his grandparents. 'Fern Hill' is a hymn to that world. The last verse is quoted often, at least in part:

> *Now I was young and easy under the apple boughs,*
> *About the lilting house and happy as the grass was green . . .*
> *Time held me green and dying*
> *Though I sang in my chains like the sea.*

Adventures in the Kitchen

It would be a rare child that hadn't a secret ambition. Mine was to be a cook. I suspect that it was inspired by a book, even though I couldn't read at the time.

The book was let loose by the people who concocted Royal Baking Powder. It contained wonderful pictures – in colour, of course – depicting a bewildering array of cakes and buns and pies and biscuits and other confections.

Believe it or not, every recipe contained some measure of Royal Baking Powder. And so at a tender age I became acquainted with the cunning of advertising.

On mature reflection, I decided not to become a cook; there was enough suffering in the world already. Many years later in New Zealand, I met a young man whose ambition to become a cook had been similarly inhibited.

He was afraid he might poison people. Nevertheless, he persevered. Shortly before I met him, he had been in charge of a banquet in the Beehive, the government building in Wellington.

It wasn't an ordinary affair: the guests were the British royal family. And for about a week afterwards, my newfound friend listened to the news in trepidation lest he had poisoned the Queen.

My decision not to become a cook didn't prevent me from watching my mother and her friends at their pots and pans. Without trying very hard, I picked up a fair idea of the craft.

Peter Langan, who had the most fashionable restaurant in London until his tragic death, had a similarly informal education. Cooking fascinated him – and he spent much of his childhood and boyhood in the kitchen of the family's hotel in Clarecastle.

I especially enjoyed the making of jam. This was in an age when wild fruit didn't go to waste.

'Scum' now has a bad significance; in my childhood, it was a good word. Small boys, including myself, loved to skim it off the boiling pot with our spoons: it tasted better than the jam itself.

The filling of the black puddings was another source of delight. The puddings were put in a big pot to boil; when they were ready, they rose to the top.

Just in case, a pudding was taken out for tasting; there was never a lack of volunteers. Baking was another craft in which small boys and small girls took an active part. When the womenfolk had the kneading almost complete, the apprentices took a little piece of the dough and flattened it between their hands.

This was baked on a few coals and was called a *cístín baise* – 'a little cake of the fist'.

Samuel Johnson said: 'Oats is a food for horses in England and for people in Scotland.' I agree. Porridge wasn't part of the culture in our neck of the fields and the bogs. We cooked American maize – known locally as yellow meal – for fowl and pigs.

Maize is popular in Italy. They can have it. There are no greater food lovers in the world or no better cooks, but we all have our weaknesses.

One morning in a hotel in Florida, I ordered hominy

grits. I thought that it was potatoes and rashers; alas, it was a kind of porridge. It was horrible. By now you will gather that oats would not be my favourite food – but we will come back to that later.

I had a similar experience with muesli in a hotel in England. The name sounded good. It was like eating gravel.

I must confess that I have never enjoyed the traditional Irish breakfast. I fear this is a creation of the advertisements in the glossy magazines. As a small boy – and I haven't changed much – my idea of an Irish breakfast embodied fried potatoes.

There is only one way to fry potatoes: boil them first. Chips are a different business: before they reach the table they have an adventurous voyage through deep fat and then they are soused in vinegar.

When Robert Mitchum was in Kerry helping to make *Ryan's Daughter*, he fell in love with the 'traditional Irish dinner'. This, of course, was bacon and cabbage and potatoes. It was traditional – but only in farmers' houses.

It was a conservative meal for the most conservative people west of India – or anywhere else. Robert Mitchum didn't have to endure it six days a week. The working classes were more resourceful: they varied their diet.

You might get an omelette on Friday while the farmers were dining on ling. This was a kind of dried fish. It was sold in long strips. It had been steeped for several days before being boiled. It was still awful.

It would have been excellent for half-soling shoes or mending cracks in wooden buildings.

The bacon served up on most rural tables was of poor quality. Sometimes it came from old sows.

There was a man in our locality who was famous as a poet and a wit. He worked off and on with farmers, and therein hangs a tale. One evening, the woman of the house asked him to say grace for himself and his three comrades. He did:

> Oh God *above*,
> So *full of Love*,
> *Take pity on us four*,
> *And send us mate*
> *That we can ate*,
> *And take away the boar*.

Maybe some morning I will enjoy the traditional Irish breakfast. I am looking forward to the sloe-eyed *cailín* playing the harp at the fireside.

Nevertheless, life goes on and those advertisements in the glossy magazines continue to mystify me. Have you ever started the day with soda farls and honey? Strangest of all in those Bord Fáilte concoctions is the absence of stress on tea.

No people are more dedicated to the leaf than the Irish. You know the saying: '*Marbh le tae agus marbh gan é*' – 'Dying from tea and dying without it.'

I didn't much like tea when I was a child. We small boys preferred cocoa: we looked on tea as a drink for girls. In that generation, there was a tin of Van Houten's in every house.

They were a huge firm. Political upheavals in West Africa put them out of business. Fry's filled the vacuum. Their factory in Rathmore was a boon to the economy of Sliabh Luachra.

There was a drink popular in my childhood that still mystifies me. I do not know whence it came or whither it vanished. It was called bees' wine. It was kept in big glass jars that had contained boiled sweets such as bulls' eyes.

It had nothing whatever to do with bees but little pieces of yeast in it looked like them. Every house in our neighbourhood had some. We were assured that it was great for the health. Young and old drank it.

It could produce strange effects: people fell from bicycles – and bicycles fell from people. Slowly, a fear grew that it was to some degree alcoholic. The strange wine disappeared.

The most common form of bread in rural Kerry in my childhood was called simply 'white bread'. It was made from white flour. This flour became very scarce during World War Two and, like tea, it was sold on the black market at outrageous prices.

Steak, of course, is deemed by many Irish people as essential in keeping body and soul together. And therein lies a little story. One night when my mother and her coven were discussing food, the different ways of cooking steak came up.

One woman said to my father: 'Mick, how do you like your steak?' And he said 'Any way but rare.'

I suspect that my abhorrence of porridge in any shape or form went back to the days when I was incarcerated in a boarding school in the woodlands of East Cork.

As we went to Mass about six in the morning, we could see the plates of porridge already in position in the refectory. It wasn't an appetising breakfast almost an hour later.

One time long ago I was editing a magazine that carried

a cookery column – and on an occasion when the expert didn't deliver, I had to rush into the breach. I wrote about what I knew best: how to fry trout. 'To prevent fragmentation, roll in flour – the trout, not yourself.'

The Changing Seasons

Sometimes in the early days of the year a fragment from Coleridge pops up on my mind's screen:

The time is a month from the moon of May,
And the spring comes slowly up this way.

The great poet was then living in the hills of Somerset; he could have written the same words in Kerry.

The seasons in these islands are not clearly defined and there is little that we can do about it.

The Cheltenham Festival provides an example. I have been there in blizzards and on days so warm that people were sleeping in the sun.

The calendar isn't the best guide to the seasons: plants and birds are more reliable. The jackdaws usually start building nests in late December; the increase in the light, almost imperceptible though it may be, stimulates them.

To see them going about their work is always encouraging: you know that the year has turned. It is still Winter on the calendar but the light is growing.

The frost and the snow may come but the earth is stirring. You will see plants peep up through the snow – because the snow has sheltered the soil.

The broad bean is a wonderful battler: it is a great sight to see it come up in the most bitter weather. The experts will tell you that it isn't really a bean at all – we will skip that.

The frost cannot prevail against it and the snow, as I hinted, is its ally. *'Faba'* is the Latin for 'bean' – and so you see whence came the word 'fabulous'.

There are many signs to tell you that Spring has been declared; there was an especial symbol in my heartland.

When you come to the summit of the road from Abbey-feale to Castle Island, you will experience a famous view. Below you lies a great saucer-valley. People with a romantic turn of mind call it 'the Heart of the Kingdom'.

Bertie Ahern says that it is his favourite sight in the whole world. I suspect that he has an even greater favourite: the sight of Fine Gael and Labour on the opposition benches.

The south-east rim of the valley is where fabled Sliabh Luachra begins – only God knows where it will end. That too is another story.

Up there on nights in late March and early April, you will see a sight that will stay with you forever. People burn the heather in strips to make way for new grass. At night the glow of those fires burning on the horizon pierces the soul.

This is about the time for the coming of the swallows. We tend to forget that the swifts and the martins come too. The cuckoo may come, though the weather is inclement.

Indeed the bitter weather frequently experienced at this time is called 'Scaraveen na gCuach' – 'the harsh weather of the cuckoos'. 'Scaraveen' is probably a corruption of 'Garbh Shíon'.

The cuckoo is not a great singer; indeed, he can hardly

sing at all. Yet he was William Wordsworth's favourite bird. 'Oh cuckoo,' he wrote, 'shall I call thee bird or but a wandering voice?'

If the weather is clement, the early potatoes should be peeping above the ground in April. Their stalks are delicate and woefully vulnerable to the frost – it can turn a lovely green garden into a horrible brown mess overnight.

May is many people's favourite month. It is said that if you can cover three daisies with your hand, Summer has arrived.

It is also the month when a lot of turf is cut in the pubs – and some in the bogs.

By now the sound of the forage harvester is heard on the land: silage-making has commenced.

The habitat of the corncrake is disappearing. Once his voice was as much a part of early Summer as that of the farmers complaining about the price of milk.

The championships are now under way in Hurling and Gaelic Football. The voices of Mícheál Ó Muircheartaigh and Marty Óg Morrissey try to make up for the loss of the corncrake.

May is the time for growth. You can have frost at night – and the growth is not so much from the heat as from the increase of light.

'A wet and windy May fills the barns with corn and hay.' There is another proverb: 'Don't cast a clout 'til May be out.'

There is a deep truth in that second saying: Summer begins in June. There is growth in May but it is piecemeal; in June, it is spectacular – you almost believe that you can see it under your eyes.

And certainly it is visible: if, for example, you inspected your garden in the morning, you might find it difficult to believe your eyes in the evening.

This is especially true of the potato garden: the stalks may grow as much in a day as in a week in May.

Now you are looking forward to the first taste of the new potatoes. In a good year, that first taste should come about the last week in June. It is a marvellous time mark; it goes far beyond potatoes.

You might say that in a special way it is a kind of new year. For the first time, you are tasting the new fruits of the earth. The old potatoes are of course flourier, but they cannot compare with the fresh new taste of the Epicures or the British Queens or the May Queens. With butter and a pinch of salt, you have a dish too good for most kings.

In places where the Gaelic language is long-since vanished, you can still hear the old prayer: '*Go mbeirimíd beo ar an am seo arís.*'

The travelling people need no telling when your early potatoes are ready. I recall an occasion when a sweet little child of the Sheridan tribe came to me bearing a shining, newly-made tin can: 'In the honour of God, Connie, will you fill this for me. We're gone dry inside in us for the want of a spud.'

The year goes on. The farmers are well aware when the corn is almost ready for cutting – the wood pigeons see to that.

September brings another kind of harvest – for some a harvest gained, for others a harvest lost. It is the culmination of the year for the Gaelic Athletic Association. It brings glory and it brings heartbreak. Sport is a hard mistress.

The swallows and the swifts and the martins are preparing to depart. And someone is likely to ask: 'Where did the swallows assemble when there were not telephone wires?' They assembled on rooftops.

October is a month for payback; it is the month for ripening. The potatoes are at their best; it is time for potato cake. The apples are at their sweetest; it is time to make pies.

November at times is dank and dark; at other times, it is soft and bright. The year is dying. 'The hedges,' as D. H. Lawrence wrote, 'show the birds' nests no longer worth hiding.'

And yet in some ways it is a friendly month. The hedges provide the birds with a profusion of wild berries. The earth is moist; worms and snails are above the ground.

The leaves are falling but the berries of the mountain ash are at their brightest red. Now there is little traffic in the fields. Those hares that had been in the woods come out and make their forms in open ground.

Rabbits enjoy the long nights. They can spend more time out of their burrows.

In my local river the first flood in November brings salmon up from the ocean. They went down as fingerlings; they return as adults after two or three years in the Arctic Ocean.

They are travelling up to breed in the shallow waters where they were born.

December is the darkest month – and the brightest: people are looking forward to the turn of the year. And within a few weeks, the jackdaws will be building. The cycle starts all over again.

AN OLD FRIEND

His name in the electoral register was Michael Sugrue. His nickname was 'Mac', pronounced in the Gaelic way as 'Mock'. He was so much a part of our community in Castle Island that some people never knew his proper name.

I always called him Mikey; we were the closest of friends since our days in the primary school. He is no longer in this mortal world – and yet if I went home tomorrow, I would expect to see him perched in his usual corner in McGillicuddy's Bar in the heart of the Latin Quarter.

Mikey had many traits. Among them was the insatiable desire for the limelight – he was the unshyest person that I ever knew. When, for example, a circus called for volunteers for some act, you could bet that he would be the first into the ring.

This obsession with being the focus of attention reached its Everest in circumstances that could have had a tragic outcome. This was back in the early seventies, when bombs were being planted in many parts of these islands.

This one Saturday, a suspicious-looking parcel was spotted in the Railway Station in Killarney. Experts came from the army in Cork. It was a bomb. They defused it.

On the following Monday evening, a box was spotted in a doorway in Castle Island. The gardaí came – all three of them. Of course a crowd gathered.

It is an odd fact of life that people will sometimes allow

their curiosity to overcome their sense of self-protection. I have seen it for myself in Dublin and in Belfast. It happened that night in Castle Island.

The gardaí had difficulty in restraining them. Mikey arrived and forced his way through the crowd. It took all three gardaí to hold him back. He kept shouting that he had been trained to defuse bombs in the LDF.

The gardaí summoned two colleagues from Tralee. Mikey was hauled down to the barracks and kept there until the experts arrived. The 'bomb' was a hoax – it was just as well.

Mikey, I need hardly tell you, was in his element in the local dance hall; invariably, he was the first out on the dance floor.

In that generation, it was not uncommon for the local dances to end in a fight – it was part of the culture. The fights usually spilled out onto the street; thus, one night Mikey found himself on the verge of a fracas which was not of his making. A garda arrived on the scene; the combatants scattered; Mikey was left on his own.

The garda was a newcomer to our town; he asked our hero for his name and address. 'Michael Sugrue, the Bakery.' 'You're not living in a bakery.' 'I'm sleeping in the oven.'

The garda was not amused – and so Mikey was hauled up before the district court. He was charged with failing to give his proper address. Of course he had no solicitor – he wished to hold centre stage.

He explained that his bedroom was the place where the bread had been baked. The judge wasn't over-impressed: he imposed a penalty of five pounds.

I can still see the headline in the *Kerryman*. How could I forget it? 'Man Fined for Sleeping in Oven'. From all this, you may begin to suspect that Mikey wasn't the full shilling, or even the full sixpence.

You would be a way out: he had a very bright mind and he was a great reader. He was totally honest and a most diligent worker, no matter what job he undertook.

I know because we often worked together. His love of the limelight was his only failing, if you could call it that. It manifested itself even in the national school, an area where most of us did our best to keep a very low profile.

One day at our history lesson, he was asked how did Wolfe Tone meet his death. The politically correct answer at the time was that the perfidious British had put strychnine in his food.

Of course Mikey knew that, but he said, 'He poisoned himself with a banana skin.' The teacher said, 'Come up here and I'll give you banana skins.'

Mikey loved Rugby. He should have been a good player but he didn't reach his peak until late in his career. He was about five foot nine. He looked skinny in his street clothes but he was a bodybuilder.

He was hard and strong and had a good turn of foot. His trouble on the Rugby field came from his craving for attention. He tended to forget that a team is composed of fifteen players.

One day in a game against the London Metropolitan Police, he took his obsession to a new height. He fielded a ball just on our twenty-five-yard line and almost on the touchline. He should have moved a few yards infield to improve the angle and kick for touch. Instead, he set off across the pitch parallel to the endline. A newcomer to our team shouted 'Back him up!'

Our scrum-half, young but pitch-wise, said: 'There's no need. He'll be back.' And so he was. In the meantime, he had got to within a few yards of the far touchline.

When he returned after a voyage of about a hundred and thirty yards, he put the ball in touch at the spot whence he had set out.

To watch Mikey preparing for a game was a fascinating experience. He began by taking off all his clothes. Then came the rubbing.

He had to be vigorously anointed from neck to ankles with a wicked concoction called Wintergreen. At last the first item of clothing, if you could call it that, was donned – a blue bathing trunks.

Next came the shorts. You may think that the jersey came next; it wasn't that way at all. There was a kind of corset to be put on and laced. This was no easy task – this item was known as a harness.

And then came the jersey, in red and white and blue, the colours of the first French Republic. Now the ankles had to be strapped – a complicated process.

Then the stockings were pulled on, then the garters, and at long last came the beloved Cotton Oxfords. Then Mikey was ready to give his all for Castle Island RFC.

Mikey was over thirty when he began to appreciate that Rugby was a team game. At an age when most players are thinking about retirement, he was reaching his peak and he achieved local immortality in a game that passed into folklore.

It was the final of the Galwey–Foley Cup, the oldest and most prestigious competition in West Munster. We were at home to Tralee – it wasn't so much a local derby as a local Grand National.

We lost our out-half in about the tenth minute. There were no subs in those days. We were almost constantly on the defensive. About fifteen minutes from the end, we got a try in a breakout. The pressure on us was then even greater.

About three minutes from the end, Mikey caught a kick-ahead about fifteen yards from our line and very close to touch. He shifted infield a little to kick.

A voice from the crowd shouted, 'Go Mac, go!' And he went: he flew up along by the touchline like a swallow, crossed at the corner flag and touched down behind the posts.

Life went on. Mikey, the ultimate free spirit, surprised us all by taking unto himself a wife – a lovely girl who was hardly half his age. He retired from Rugby but acquired a kind of fame in another field.

He had a great imagination and was never caught for an answer. One Friday night there was a debate about a word that had appeared that day in the *Kerryman*. It was in an advertisement for our club's annual dinner dance.

It included the menu. It began with the word 'consommé'. When Mikey arrived, the question was put to him. He took a good sup out of his pint and put down the glass and said: 'Ignorance is a terrible thing. Doesn't everyone know that consommé is a roast bonham stuffed with rice.'

We miss you, Mikey. We all loved you. You gave to the world more than it ever gave to you.

Unsung Heroes

It is gone now. It was unique in these islands. To find a counterpart you would have to search in Africa or in Asia.

It was a kind of village made up of dwellings that you could hardly call houses – they were huts. They were built of mud and stone and roofed with thatch. Most of them consisted of no more than two rooms.

This settlement was called Pound Road; it was part of my local town, Castle Island. Big families grew up in those dwellings. How, only God knew – and there were times when He must have blinked His eyes and scratched His head.

The people of Pound Road had running water – in a stream about two hundred yards away and from a pump where a bucket took twenty minutes to fill. They were poor, desperately poor – and yet they were better off than many of their neighbours.

Many of the woman worked at jobs that others would deem beneath them, such as cleaning houses and doing laundry. And they were all experts at what you might call low cuisine: they valued parts of meat of which most people were blissfully unaware.

Sheep's heads, for example, made excellent brawn. A cow's tail takes three hours to boil but is well worth the wait.

Some of the younger women took the train to Cahirciveen to work at the mackerel harvest. Many of the older men in my youth had been in the Great War: they had pensions – small, but useful in bad times.

The most famous of them all, the unofficial Lord Mayor of Pound Road, hadn't been to war – he had been born with bad eyesight. Mikey Conway was of average height and strongly built; except for one day at the barber's, I never saw him without his cap.

As far as I know he could neither read nor write, but he was marvellously articulate. In England he would have been called the town crier; in our idiom he was the bellman. He performed a very useful service, not least for the county council.

When, for instance, something went wrong with the reservoir, he would inform the citizens that the water would be cut off for a certain time. He did this by ringing a big metal bell and speaking in a powerful voice.

Mikey didn't so much speak as mould every word. And on Sundays you could see him at Chapel Lane Corner announcing events to come or advertising lost animals. 'A roan heifer belonging to Thady Twomey strayed from the fair here last week. If anyone has seen her or her equals, report to me or to the Garda barracks.'

Whenever Mikey encountered an unfamiliar word, he substituted a word of his own. Thus, in announcing a production by Anew McMaster, *Oedipus Rex* became *Oedipus the Wreck*. When you come to think of it, he wasn't far wrong.

When a budding young entrepreneur decided to get into the bell-ringing profession, he didn't fare too well. His name was Seán Costello; on his first evening as a town crier, he was going up the middle of the street when he met Mikey coming down.

When they met, Mikey uttered a basic principle of socialism: 'One man, one job.' He then hit Seán smartly over the head with his bell. When Seán recovered and got to his feet, he turned to a bystander and said, 'Billy, you saw that . . . '

The bystander, the famous jockey Billy Murphy, then retired, said, 'I did, Seán – and 'twas the grace of God that he missed you.'

Mikey fancied himself as the arbitrator of all disputes in Pound Road – by force if necessary. One night he heard a commotion outside in the Cooleen, the little piece of ground that was the plaza in Pound Road.

He rushed out and saw his wife's sister stretched on the ground in the middle of the crowd. 'Who hit that woman?' he asked. 'I did,' said a small hardy man called John C. Brosnan who had been a champion boxer in the British army. 'Then,' said Mikey, 'she must have deserved it.'

Mikey's eldest son, Georgie, emigrated to Huddersfield, joined the army when war broke out and served under Field Marshal Montgomery. Thus he was in the thick of the action when the famous battle of El Alamein, the final duel between Montgomery and General Rommel, got under way.

On the first day it was all the talk on the wireless: there were bulletins by the hour. That evening when Mikey arrived at the street parliament at the Market House, someone said: 'I suppose you're all worried about Georgie.'

'There's no need to worry about our Georgie. He don't care about the Germans or the Eyetalians or even Rommel himself. Before he went to England, he spent three years with the farmers.'

The Battle of El Alamein ran its course – and soon after it ended, Georgie came home on furlough. 'He's a humble lad,' said Mikey at the street parliament. 'He ate his dinner above with us today – and only a week ago he had his legs under Montgomery's table.'

Perhaps the most celebrated story about Mikey is set in the bog. The cast was composed of himself, the afore-mentioned Georgie, and his second son Charlie. It was Charlie's maiden voyage to the bog, and therein hangs the tale.

About half past ten he was dispatched to bring the water for the lunch. 'A quarter to eleven came and eleven o'clock came,' said Mikey, 'but Charlie never came. I had to go and look for him.'

He went on, 'There was my poor son and he wandering up and down, hither and over, north and south, east and west. God help us, blindness is a terrible affliction – only for he falling into the well he'd never find it.'

A man who was as famous as Mikey Conway lived a few doors away; his name on the register was Thomas Prendi-ville – most people knew him simply as Tom Bawn. He was a small, roundy man and, like Mikey, was never seen without his cap.

He had spent much of his early life working in a stable near Mallow. World War II did no good for racing in these islands. Tom came home. There was no work for him; he signed on for the dole.

He registered as a 'jockey and horse trainer'. A few days later he was drawing stones from a quarry with a Clydesdale that stood almost eighteen hands. At stopping time that evening he told the foreman he was taking early retirement. We met that night in Hussey's pub.

And soon he complained to me: "Twas a terrible comedown for a man who wore silk.' Somehow he scraped a few pounds together and bought a Baby Ford. It was so ancient that it might have been one of the first off the production line in Dearborn.

The experts will tell you that the Baby Ford was the best car ever made; Tom Bawn's sweet chariot was a proof. With his son, a young man known as Sonny Bawn, he set up as a fish vendor.

Sonny was tall, at least compared to his father. He had dark-brown hair and eyes and sallow skin; he was very shy. He was never trained as a motor mechanic but he could make that Baby Ford sing. On Wednesday nights he and Tom set out to West Kerry to buy fish.

They bypassed Dingle; there you had to deal with middlemen. They went ten miles beyond it to a little harbour called Cuasabhádaigh. There they bought from the brave men who fished from canoes – or *naomhógs*, as they called them.

By the time Tom and Sonny got back to Castle Island, they had travelled over a hundred miles. Thursday was the occasion for the market in our town. Tom set out his table at Chapel Lane Corner – about as close to the middle of the town as you could get.

If they had fish left over on Friday, they set off north into the hill-country. On Friday night the two fish vendors enjoyed a quiet celebration. They adjourned to one of the pubs in the Latin Quarter – usually McGillicuddy's, Hussey's or Cronin's.

When Tom had a few half-ones inside him, it was easy to persuade him to sing. He had a lovely voice and great feeling for a song. Most of his songs are forgotten. There was one I especially cherished. It told about a girl who planned to dress up as a boy and go to sea with her sailor lover.

The song begins:

> Adieu, lovely Mary, I am bound now to leave you
> For the far-distant Indies my course for to steer,
> And though I know that my absence will grieve you,
> I'll still be back home in the spring of the year.

She persists, and he says:

> Your delicate waist strong winds won't resist, love,
> The waves and the tempests, the sleet and the snow.
> Your dainty white feet to the top mast won't climb, love.
> Stay at home, lovely Mary, to the sea do not go.

Sonny was a handy player on the mouth organ but didn't accompany his father. Folk singers like to be on their own. It is the same all over the world. Sonny wasn't into Irish folk music: he played the popular tunes of the day.

They too were a kind of folk music. We liked such songs as 'The Isle of Capri' and 'The Red River Valley' and, of course, 'South of the Border'.

In my youth I took Mikey and Tom and Sonny for granted; now I see them as unsung heroes.

ORWELL'S OWN GOAL

George Orwell is high among my heroes, but he wasn't infallible – he perpetrated an own goal when Moscow Dynamo visited Britain soon after World War II. Not all their games against local clubs were things of beauty and a joy forever. The hostility on the pitch led Orwell to suspect that Football games between nations were more likely to cause tension than to ease it.

It would be idle to suggest that the World Cup can eventually bring about peace between men, but it is a step in the right direction. When the concept was first mooted, approval was less than universal. Indeed, there was widespread indifference. In Britain, this indifference amounted to something akin to hostility. The Empire was still a monolith on which the sun never went down; the winds of change were far away. The English and the Scots vied with each other for the honour of having created Soccer; both tribes seemed to regard other nations as pretenders. Nonetheless, the tournament went on, even if it would be a slight exaggeration to call it a World Cup.

There was an obvious explanation for England's reluctance to join the new tournament: they were unbeaten on their own soil – and rather arrogantly deemed themselves world champions. They may not have been aware that South America was becoming a Soccer heartland. The game was developed there by English and Scots and Germans who worked to bring the Continent into the industrial world.

The World Cup began with a whisper in 1930. Uruguay beat Argentina in the final. It was played in Montevideo before a crowd of ninety thousand. Italy beat Czechoslovakia in the final of 1934 before fifty thousand people in Rome. The tournament was taking on an intercontinental flavour. Italy won again in 1938: they beat Hungary in the final before ninety-five thousand people in Paris. Then war intervened.

The Cup restarted in 1950. The finals of that year are remembered for many reasons, not least the game between England and the US. The Americans appeared to be no more than a ragbag of mercenaries, but they won by the only goal. It was as sensational as if Kerry had knocked Tipperary out of the Munster Hurling Championship. The game was not broadcast, and when the 1–0 scoreline came to Britain on the wire, it was deemed a mistake. One paper published the result as England 10, US 0. There was no knock-out that year: the last round was played on a league system. Uruguay beat Brazil in the decisive tie before 200,000 in Rio de Janeiro. And so a nation of only three million people had won its second World Cup. Back in Uruguay, seven people died during the broadcast; more died during the celebrations that followed.

The Cup was well on the way. It needed someone of Superman stature to stamp it indelibly on the imagination of the world. He came in the form of a seventeen-year-old Brazilian who played against Sweden in the finals of 1958. His name was Juan Nascimento; he has long gone into folklore as Pele. His goal in the final against Sweden hinted that the skills of Football were entering new territory.

It also unleashed a new species of expert – the Football psychologist. Several of them joyfully seized on Pele as a specimen of the new-age footballer. His marvellous coalition of reflexes and coordination was the product of the culture inherent in the rainforest. Pele was translating into Football his heritage from a long line of ancestors who hunted and fished for a living. And the time had come when South America would dominate the world of Football.

It was a relief to discover that Pele came from a family of people long settled in the city of Rosario. His father may have hunted and fished in the rainforest, but he had made his living as a professional footballer.

Life went on: Brazil delighted the Football psychologists by winning the next World Cup. They beat Czechoslovakia in the final. That tournament was held in Chile. The next finals would be held in England and would test the rainforest theory.

The Summer of 1966 was a watershed: most of the games were televised to most parts of the world. It effected a quiet revolution in our island: it opened windows and blew away cobwebs – and implanted Soccer in almost every parish. The Football world will remember it not least for the game between Italy and North Korea. The Italian team included such icons as Albertosi and Facchetti and Mazzola, but lost by the only goal. To the present day, thirty-five years later, it is unwise to mention that game in Italy.

That year's final is generally deemed the best ever. England beat West Germany by four goals to two. The third 'goal' was decisive; it wasn't a goal at all. I know Germans who are still bitter about it. The full video of the final is often shown; I have lost count of how often I have watched it – and would do so again. I remember it for the good Football and the exemplary chivalry – and, most of all, for the display of Bobby Moore. He was England's captain in more than name: never did anyone exemplify more clearly Ernest Hemingway's 'grace under pressure'. The fates were unkind to Bobby, God rest him; I will remember him as the Golden Man of midsummer 1966.

The finals were staged in Spain in 1982. I was stationed for a while in Segovia, in the hill country fifty miles north of Madrid. The land in between witnessed the fiercest fighting in the Civil War. There an Irish poet, Charlie Donnelly, lost his life fighting fascism. He left behind an immortal line – 'even the olives are bleeding'. I thought about him every day as we drove up and down and was glad that he hadn't died in vain.

A great many people will remember Spain '82 for the meeting of France and West Germany in the semi-final. The game was played in Seville. There was a heatwave in the Western Mediterranean. I expected it to be played at a very slow pace – stop-go-stop-go. It was go-go-go. The burning night seemed to create a kind of madness. That brilliant French team were at their peak. West Germany had been world champions in 1974. The Football that night was enthralling. The atmosphere was overpowering. The teams were level at ninety minutes. France lost a two-goal lead in extra time. West Germany won the shoot-out. One thing marred a marvellous occasion – Harald Schumacher's 'tackle' that left Patrick Batiston unconscious and at death's door. The German keeper should have been sent off. France didn't even get a penalty. Nevertheless, that meeting has gone into folklore as one of the greatest games of any kind ever experienced. It has got almost as much coverage as the Battle of Waterloo.

Back in the hotel room in Madrid, I felt helpless to express the essence of that epic. I could summon up Shakespeare and Dante and Tolstoy himself – it would be in vain. I did what I could and sent it to the *Evening Press*.

West Germany had only three days to recover from their ordeal. Italy cruised through the final.

The Republic, of course, battled their way to Italy and the islands and to the United States – the present wave danced their way to the Far East. It is easy to be optimistic at a remove of time; the good feeling at the announcement of the draw is now diminishing. It is an old belief in Football that a corner should get past the first defender – in the World Cup finals we must get past our first opponents.

We will do well to draw with Cameroon. That would be an excellent start. If we take Iran as a benchmark, Saudi Arabia are formidable. A win over them is essential. Against Germany, we can hope for no more than a draw.

Incidentally, the 1966 game between England and West Germany, plus that between France and West Germany in Seville, indicated that George Orwell may have got it wrong.

Magill, June 2002

GOING IN HARD

There was a time – and it isn't long ago – when attending a game of Rugby could get a member of the GAA cast into exterior darkness. And it isn't too long since a Catholic priest in the fair county of Kerry proclaimed that attendance at all-night dances carried the penalty of excommunication.

Those wild and whirling words had little import. The ban on such 'foreign' games as Rugby and Soccer was a different kettle of Footballs. Soccer then was hardly even in swaddling clothes in my neck of the bogs – Rugby was the big threat to faith and morals.

Nevertheless, many pure Gaels seldom missed an opportunity of watching the Devil's game. Of course they drew a line between watching and attending; this wasn't difficult – most provincial pitches had low walls or no walls at all. And even high walls weren't much of a deterrent: trees and rooftops served as grandstands, if at some risk to life and limb. The young people of today can hardly believe that this was part of our culture a generation ago. The coming of television played a big part in blowing it all away.

One aspect of Rugby intrigued those who watched from outside – of course it was the scrum. Many a time I was asked what was the point in a huddle of men with their heads down and their backsides up. Incidentally, those backsides shouldn't be up – but that's another story.

How could I explain? I would need to go back to the middle of the nineteenth century.

You could write a book on the history of the scrum – doctorates have been given for less. When you read some accounts of early Football games, you will begin to understand the scrum.

'Masses of men drove into each other, while the fleeter of foot waited on the outskirts.' This, believe it or not, is from an account of a Gaelic Football game. This hints that there wasn't much difference between Rugby and Gaelic in those days.

There wasn't – until Michael Cusack picked what he deemed the better elements of Soccer and Rugby and created Gaelic Football. I need hardly add that but for the invention of the pneumatic bladder, neither Soccer not Gaelic would have been possible. Rugby would have continued in a crude form because it was a carrying rather than a kicking game.

Let us return to the scrum. Why did it become an essential part of Rugby? The reason was simple: when those masses of men drove into each other, the ball, more often than not, didn't come out. Thus came the scrum – a limited number of players faced each other to win the ball. It was designed as a means of restarting the game. Like some things that had a simple beginning – parliaments, for example – it grew and grew. And eventually it was much more than a means of restarting the game.

The forwards, the foot soldiers who hewed wood and carried water, began to ask themselves why the cavalry should have all the best songs. Of course there was more to it than that. Coaches began to perceive that the scrum could be a fertile source of attack. Thus came the wheel: the forwards who had won the ball could turn the scrum until it was back to front. Then you could pick up the ball and start a handling move or bring it away by dribbling.

The wheel became a favourite tactic in Scotland, due in no small part to that country's abominable climate. Dribbling is a better bet than handling when the pitch is heavy and the wind and the rain are at large. Thus the cry of 'Feet, Scotland, feet' was intended to terrify the Sassenachs and other inferior breeds. The scrum could also be used to make possession a dubious boon.

One of the basic principles in Rugby is: win the ball going forward, if only by an inch. When your pack lose the ball, you can make life difficult for your opponents in various ways. You can crab the scrum by wheeling it a little and thus make a clean heel almost impossible. You can time your shove so that the heel is slow and hard to control. I have suggested enough.

Carwyn Jones, the greatest of Welsh philosophers, was an expert on the scrum – as an out-half he had cause. He didn't fancy the ball coming back to him after trickling out of the scrum. And it was he who popularised the concept of channel A and B and C. When the ball emerges between the lock's feet, it is in channel A; when it comes out between the feet of a wing-forward, it is in channel B or C. Channel A is the main door; channels B and C would be understood by Liam Lawlor. The scrum in the old days was composed of two packs who were in 3–2–3 formation. Now, 3–4–1 is almost statutory.

The scrum may change but one truth will never change – and this I can guarantee from long experience. The first scrum in a game is of enormous importance: if you can force your opponents back even a centimetre, the feeling is great for the spirit.

If you can maintain this superiority for eighty minutes, you are almost certain to end up in the winners' dressing room. The scrum, I need hardly add, is dangerous territory; therein occur most of the game's serious injuries. The risks could be minimised if all behaved – unfortunately, life isn't that way. Most of these injuries are caused by scrumduggery. The props are the principal offenders: they try to lift their opponents or pull them down. This, of course, is illegal – but most referees are not expert in the morality and the mechanics of the front row. Few forwards take up the whistle: this is especially true of props – when their playing days are over, they are content to watch from the shore.

About thirty years ago, what seemed a simple change in the laws affected the game profoundly. Until then when the ball went loose after a tackle, it had to be played with the foot. Now, the player who has been tackled tries to retain the ball and place it between his body and his own team.

'Laying back' usually enables a colleague to pick up and form the apex of a loose scrum. In the old days, if a loose scrum resulted after a tackle, it was a ruck – because the ball was on the ground. Most loose scrums now are mauls – the ball is in the hand. The change in the law has made it much easier to retain possession. It is quite common to see a team retain the ball for six or more loose scrums in a row.

This is one of the factors that is making the game less attractive – in this aspect it resembles Rugby League. The laws governing the scrum are satisfactory; they need only to be applied.

The game's other set piece, the line-out, is now a joke in dubious taste. Lifting had become so prevalent that the lawmakers decided to make it legal. With such thinking, you could legalise steroids, not to mention the mugging of old ladies – and even young ladies. It is true that the line-out had become a competition in lifting – but there was a simple remedy. Persistent offenders could have been sent to the line – that would have put manners on them. The line-out as we know it now demands neither athleticism nor coordination: the expert has only to catch the ball, uncontested.

Why must the hooker throw in the ball? Seemingly this practice began in New Zealand – other countries slavishly followed. The ball could be thrown in by a winger or a loose forward – or by the scrum-half.

Let us return to the scrum; I recall a nice cartoon in this context. Two young lassies are watching a scrum. One says: 'All those poor fellows are fighting for the ball – and that horrid number 9 has it all the time.'

Magill, March 2002

The Irish Dilemma

One day a few weeks ago a train set out from Cavan for Limerick. This was less than remarkable; it had been doing so for years. Its journey proved undramatic: no budding Jesse James or Ned Kelly halted it. This made sense – it wasn't carrying gold bullion or wealthy passengers. It was transporting a cargo of gypsum. The surprising aspect is that this was its final journey.

Some Great White Chief had decided that it was cheaper to use the roads. This decision might have made sense a half-century ago; today it passes understanding. In the meantime, we have had a superabundance of evidence to show that we should be building more railways rather than closing them down.

Those responsible for 'rationalising' our rail system did the state no service. There was a time when the network served every nook and many crannies in this island; today several parts of this country lack feasible public transport. The evidence of the 'rationalisation' is all around us. When, for example, you see a big, heavily laden truck in Dawson Street, you wonder who is in charge of Dublin's transport policy.

Freight clogs the roads and adds to the hazards. It would be sensible to put as much freight as possible on the railway and to encourage people to travel by train. The current train service is not particularly attractive, especially at weekends. There is little joy in standing or sitting on your baggage in the train all the way from Heuston to Tralee. It was bad enough to close down the branch lines; uprooting them was a destruction of invaluable capital. Nobody shouted 'Stop!'

It is well over thirty years since I began campaigning for the railways. I did so as an activist of the Labour Party – and in the *Kerryman* and the *Evening Press*. I was in good company with Myles na Gopaleen. He wrote: 'The railways do not pay – so they tell us. It is as well that they do not apply the same criterion to the roads.' It would be too much to hope that some government would do an about-turn and restore our rail system to its former glory. It could, however, desist from destroying branch lines and put more trains – freight and passenger – on the lines that remain.

Similarly, the state of our waters is a terrible indictment of a succession of governments. It is a consolation that rivers and lakes cannot be 'rationalised'. Neglect, however, can go so far that reclamation can take generations. Some of our great fishing lakes are now almost dead. There are five million registered anglers in Britain; there are many more in Continental Europe. For them this country should be a promised land or, if you like, a promised water.

These good people could be our best tourist market; it wouldn't depend on the fluctuation of the dollar or fear of air travel. Our governments have been at fault in persisting with laws that impose only token penalties – but as a people we are not blameless. I recall what Sherwood Anderson, the father of modern American writing, said about the United States in the early twentieth century: 'We have taken as lovely a land as ever lay out of doors and put the old stamp of ourselves on it for keeps.'

Dublin provides all too convincing an example: it has turned its back on four rivers – the Liffey, the Tolka, the Camac and the Dodder. The Dodder is the most abused river in Western Europe – or in any part of Europe. If properly treated, it would abound in trout – and would have walks along its banks. As it is, it passes through the city almost anonymously.

Over thirty years ago, I was one of a small group who founded the Castle Island Anglers' Club – too well I know about the war against pollution. Once, in desperation, I organised what would be a mighty meeting – little did I know. I wrote to every Dáil deputy, senator, county councillor and town councillor in Kerry. A few sent their regrets. Two attended.

On another occasion I again showed my innocence. I wrote to the county council and asked them to stop allowing untreated sewage into our local river, the Maine. No answer came. One day many years later I discovered what happened that letter. On the train to an All-Ireland final I met one of the council engineers – a decent man long since gone to his reward – and he confessed that the letter had been shredded. That tells you something about the official attitude to the environment a generation ago.

It would take a big capital investment to restore the railways; our waters offer no such problem. All over the country there are clubs that do selfless work in stocking and restocking; all that we need is the political will to punish the offenders.

The year 2001 probably marked a watershed, or perhaps a tearshed, in education in the Republic. The teachers' revolt was superficially about pay: essentially it was a symptom of deep malaise. I know several bright young people – dedicated teachers – who have quit the profession. The short hours and the long holidays weren't sufficient attraction: the frustration proved too much.

It is a sad picture – and the roots are so deep that there is no easy solution. Some primary teachers have to cope – or attempt to cope – with classes that are too big: many secondary teachers must struggle with the crazy points system.

The most alarming aspect is that vocations will decline until a deeper crisis demands radical action – what kind of action, I do not know. Money will not solve this. The growth in the urban populations made overcrowding in the city primary schools almost inevitable; a succession of governments are to blame for the points' system. When Donagh O'Malley put the yellow buses on the mountain roads, they were caught with their statistics down. Entry to university should be a matter of reaching a certain level, not a competition. The points system has driven students and teachers and parents to mental breakdowns. It has made a mockery of the concept of education.

Commenting on the crisis in our national health system is a cottage industry: like the problem in education, it is so deep-seated that there is no easy solution.

Our policing is woefully inadequate; a modicum of purpose and intelligence can go a long way to remedy it. Those parts of the country that lack public transport are more or less the same parts that lack effective policing. There is an urgent need for mobile gardaí in most rural areas. They would give isolated people some measure of protection and lessen the hazards on the roads. This country had an auxiliary police force during World War II; it worked well. There is more need of such a body now, preferably made up of men and women who are familiar with their beats. The alternative is the vigilantes, many of whom are sinister people and some of whom have subversive connections.

Dublin may be the cultural capital of Europe; it is also possibly its most dangerous city. I like walking in foreign cities at hours when sensible people are in bed – but not in Dublin. It shares this honour with New York. Dublin, thankfully, has no equivalent of the old Times Square, but it is working at it. The quays at O'Connell Bridge are not places where you are likely to linger around midnight, or indeed any time of the night. This shouldn't be; there is no point in blaming the Gardaí – it is a question of numbers.

Ultimately, the blame resides with a succession of governments. This state has never had a radical government; we have had no politician with the drive and vision of Franklin Roosevelt. We have never had a New Deal: the nearest equivalent was provided by the government that came into office in 1948. Then, we enjoyed a few years of ferment. There was a whiff of revolution in the air. Politics in the Republic today is moribund.

Fianna Fáil have no philosophy; they are content to hold power. Fine Gael lost all purpose when they ignored Peter Barry and ditched Alan Dukes. The Labour Party lost the run of themselves when they won a record number of seats in the Dáil. They celebrated in the National Concert Hall. The delegates voted by an overwhelming majority to coalesce with Fianna Fáil – against tradition and common sense. That was the Bad Sunday Agreement. Many friends of mine, staunch socialists, vowed never to vote Labour again.

The alliance with the Democratic Left was another stumble in the wrong direction. It cost a decent wee girl her seat in the European Parliament. She may not have wheeled her wheelbarrow through streets broad and narrow, but that was the end of poor Bernie Malone.

There is a consolation: as a people, we haven't lost our sense of humour, even if it has a rather dark hue. The long-running decommissioning crisis is an example. Does anyone understand what the word means? Does anyone believe that the Provisional IRA will dump their lethal toys beyond reuse? We read occasionally about the disgraced former Taoiseach. If Charlie Haughey stood for the next election, he would probably head the poll – that's how disgraced he is.

Again I recall Sherwood Anderson: 'Here in America we must start thinking. We must ask ourselves who we are and where we are going.'

Magill, January 2002

In the Heat of Battle

I have never known finer people than my neighbours who survived the Great War. I wasn't born for several years after they returned from Flanders and Greece and the Middle East and the other battlegrounds. Nevertheless, we spoke the same language: the concept of the generation gap was probably the brainchild of some American scholar short of fodder for a doctorate.

The men who came back from the war resembled the survivors of the *Titanic*; they didn't allow little things to bother them. They looked on being alive as a privilege and took the days as they came. They needed no telling about life's penchant for irony: they were practised catchers in the wry.

Danny Horan was the man I knew best of the returned soldiers. We had much in common, not least our passion for Rugby.

Danny had known life in the trenches but seemed to have put it all behind him. Whenever he spoke about France, it was to sing the praises of its women. I never held that against him. He had played Rugby for our club before he went to war; back at home he was content to be our groundsman – perhaps he was tired of battle.

He was a perfectionist in all he attempted; he kept that pitch like a tennis lawn and before every game he marked it meticulously. Danny never spoke about 'marking' the pitch. He 'painted' it.

Alas, my dear friend was human, and on a very important occasion he fell from his high estate. Castle Island were to play Tralee in the final of the Galwey–Foley Cup. It was the oldest and the most prestigious trophy in West Munster. Tralee were the old enemy; the match wouldn't be so much a local Derby as a local Grand National.

The date was the last Sunday before Christmas. It was – and still is – a time fraught with danger: the lads are home from across the Irish Sea and elsewhere. Danny was out and about with his extended family on the Saturday night. Next morning his eyes weren't comrades; for once he had painted the pitch – literally.

I came to inspect it about midday, recovered from the shock, and summoned all hands on deck. The game went on and we won a famous victory.

Late that night in the midst of the celebrations I found myself alone with Danny – and he said: 'I was talking to the referee, a grand man from Cork. He asked me who painted the pitch and I told him.' I said nothing. Danny went on: 'He shook my hand and bought me a glass of whiskey and said that I should be above in Lansdowne Road.'

The men who came back from the war were the hard core of our followers in Rugby – and they were the leaders of a practice that is confined more or less to Limerick and Castle Island. Our storm troopers followed the play up and down along by the sideline, even when it was on the opposite side of the pitch. If some visiting dignitary got knocked over in the stampede, it was all part of our culture.

The returned soldiers had an especial reason for their devotion to Rugby: they didn't feel at home in the 'Gaelic'

Ireland promulgated by the extreme elements in the GAA. They felt themselves outsiders to some degree: the new Association may have been populist but it was dominated by the middle classes.

The poorer people in our community looked on Rugby as their game. This attitude was not without a smidgen of irony: Rugby in this country was generally deemed the game of those who dwelt in the upper plateaus. In the world of sport you will find that poverty and passion go hand in hand. No club ever had more fervent followers than ours. Whether it was a Cup game or a friendly, it was all the same; of course there were no friendlies in our Rugby.

I have a piquant memory of a 'friendly' between ourselves and Killarney. It tended to boil over. The interval came as a kind of truce. A woman who was famous as nurse to the local poor came onto the pitch. She was convinced that the referee wasn't fair and asked me to hit him when next he gave a penalty against us. I considered the consequences: I would be banned from Rugby for life and probably hauled up before the local court.

The first broadcast of an international game that we could get left behind it a story that has been told over and over again. It concerned three decent men who have long since gone to their eternal reward.

They lived in Chapel Lane, now gone upmarket as Church Street. Danny Sheehy was a small shopkeeper who doubled as a photographer. Bill Harrington was a butcher who doubled as an incurable innocent. Tommy Casey trebled as collector at the chapel gate, singer in the choir, and star of the local billiards team. I almost forgot that he was also a tailor – though when the fish were running, he tended to desert his tape and scissors, not to mention the thimble and needle.

Wireless sets were few then. Danny and Tommy had full houses. England were leading by two points with five minutes to go. Bill was in Danny's house. He could take no more. He went across the road to Tommy's. He got there in time to hear Ireland get what proved to be the winning score. That night at the street-corner parliament he said, 'Tommy Casey has a great wireless. Danny Sheehy's is no good at all.'

We could receive television in our neck of the woods and bogs by the time Moss Keane got his first cap. My father, God rest him, took a half-day from the creamery. He said, 'It would be a bad time for a man's horse to fall into a drain.'

The workplaces were deserted; by three o'clock there wasn't a dog on the streets. Moss's parents had never seen a Rugby game. They bought a set for the match. We were playing France in Paris. The early exchanges were hectic. His mother said, 'I'm terrified that the young lad will break a leg.' 'He might,' said his father, 'but it won't be his own.'

There is a spot in the pitch at Lansdowne Road that is known as the Castle Island corner. It is at the junction of the goal line and the touchline opposite the old Lansdowne Pavilion. Mick Doyle and Tom Doyle and Moss Keane and Mick Galwey all scored tries there in international games. The try scored by 'the young lad' was the most spectacular. On his way to the line he handed off three Scots and left them spinning on the turf. The report in the *Evening Press* said that they were rolling stones that had gathered no Moss.

When Mick Doyle got his first cap, we decided the time was right to reward Danny Horan for his long service. We arranged for the trip to Lansdowne Road and a day out with all expenses paid. We got him the best possible ticket, halfway up the East Stand and in line with the middle of the pitch. It was an exciting game. France led until five minutes from the end; then we got an equalising try. We were all in great form on the way home in the train. Danny said that he had enjoyed the best day of his life. Later that night in the bar he said to me, 'Do you know, Connie, I missed something.' I said, 'Go on.' 'I missed the running up and down.'

Magill, November 2001

FRIENDS AND ENEMIES

A few weeks ago John Joe Landers, Kerry Football icon, 'went across the river and into the trees.' His passing evoked for me a flood of memories.

It is a Sunday evening in late September 1933; I am dispatched on my trusty bike to find out who had won the All-Ireland final.

I freewheeled blithely down to Castle Island; the nearest wireless set was two miles away at the bottom of the town in the Latin quarter.

I could have found a set nearer but it would have entailed knocking at the door of some merchant who might not take kindly to me rising above my station.

I had no worry about approaching Andy Moynihan in his little shop; he was a decent man, even if he always wore his hat behind the counter. He spelled out the result with great care: Cavan had beaten Galway by 2–5 to 1–4.

As I pedalled back up the hill, I was in the company of Paul Revere, not to mention the intrepid riders of the Pony Express.

My father was pleased with the result; so were the neighbours who rambled into our house in the course of the night. They were pleased because a bond had been formed between Kerry and Cavan in the previous year.

The semi-final between them had been fixed for Tralee; Cavan made no objection. They travelled to Tralee on the Saturday and were greeted by a band and given a civic reception. It was all very civilised.

That game produced a story that seems incredible today. The Civil War had done the new state little good: communications were in a bad way. Cavan had no telephone connections; it couldn't get Radio Éireann.

On the Sunday morning a modest expedition set out by car from the town of Cavan and brought two racing pigeons with them. You can imagine the excitement back at the base as the evening wore on; it was almost dusk when the gallant birds arrived. The news was bad: Cavan had lost by a point.

The counties met again in the semi-final in 1933. Kerry travelled to Cavan. The home team won a famous victory; they went on to beat Galway in the All-Ireland final.

Cavan and Kerry met again in the final of 1937. The game ended in a draw. The experts deemed it the best exhibition of Gaelic Football ever seen.

It was memorable for another reason: the running commentary was more like a walking commentary. Radio Éireann had experimented with several commentators and found them wanting.

They called on a senior clergyman whose passion for the game almost equalled his religious fervour. No doubt it seemed a good idea at the time. Canon Hamilton talked himself into folklore.

The walking commentary was punctuated with several stops as the holy man struggled to identify the players. He didn't noticeably succeed – enthusiasm wasn't enough.

However, he got the colours of the counties right – and thus you heard that a Kerryman had got the ball and kicked it toward the Cavan goal.

This was hardly surprising and you weren't astonished

to hear that a Cavan man had got the ball and kicked it towards the Kerry goal. The good priest crowned his afternoon by giving the result incorrectly.

It wasn't altogether his fault; the game ended in confusion. Cavan seemed to have won by a last-minute point; their followers rejoiced, their counterparts mourned.

Officially the result was given as a draw; that late 'score' was deemed to have come from a throw. Many years later I met Paddy Boylan; he was adamant that he had palmed the ball cleanly.

His marker, my friend Bill Kinnerk, was equally adamant that Paddy had fouled the ball. P. D. Merigan, otherwise 'Carberry', produced a masterpiece in the *Irish Times*: 'Boylan waved the ball over the bar.'

It was the good priest's last broadcast. I suppose you could say that he was a loose canon. Micheál O'Hehir had a soft act to follow.

The replay was not a thing of beauty: Jim Smith, Cavan's brilliant full-back, was 'taken out' early; the game became bad-tempered. Kerry won by six points but did not win general admiration.

The bitterness between the counties still lingers. I have known it to erupt not only in Dublin but in London and in Boston and New York. Sometimes the argument is between men who weren't born at the time of the game.

Kerry met Galway in the final in 1938. They drew; at least that was what the referee said. Scores were level as play entered the last minute. Then Charlie O'Sullivan, star Kerry forward, posted a long ball over the bar.

The Kerry followers rejoiced; the Galway followers mourned.

Eventually a runner circulated that the result was a draw. Seemingly the referee had blown the final whistle while the ball was in flight. It was a remarkable piece of timing.

The replay also had a bizarre ending. The gremlins that inhabit Croke Park struck again. About five minutes remained when some joker in the crowd blew a long blast on a whistle. Play ceased. Galway were four points ahead. Their followers swarmed onto the pitch. The referee insisted on playing out time. The pitch was cleared, and the referee signalled for play to resume – but several of the Kerry team had departed to their dressing room in Barry's Hotel.

They were recalled; some returned. Eventually Kerry cobbled together a team. Time was played out. Kerry got a point in those few minutes. It was just as well that they didn't score enough to win.

Let us now indulge in a flashback to 1933. Kerry's satisfaction at Cavan's capture of the Sam Maguire had an obvious basis: it was a compensation to see your conquerors go all the way.

And of course it was almost an article of faith that the All-Ireland would soon return to the Kingdom. The county had achieved a four-in-a-row between 1929 and 1932 – failure in 1933 was only a slip.

Kerry were back in the mainstream in 1934 and faced up to Dublin in the semi-final in Tralee. The Kingdom's team-sheet was a litany of folk heroes. The faithful followers looked forward to a sixty-minute lap of honour in the Austin Stack Park.

For half an hour they were in raptures – Kerry were in a winning position at half-time. The second half brought a stunning change. Dublin were transformed; suddenly our gods were seen to have feet and hands of clay.

John Joe Landers was one of those gods: he had played a major part in the four-in-a-row. He was one of the few that survived the debacle and was on board when Kerry got back again to Croke Park in 1937.

Two brilliant goals would have made him man of the match in that ugly replay if the label had existed at the time. It was a great era for nicknames. Some genius rechristened John Joe as 'Purty'.

His younger brother Tim was middle-sized and rather rotund; it was almost inevitable that he was called 'Roundy'. They shared in many a triumph. Some people deemed Tim the more skilful.

That may have been so, but John Joe, who was almost six feet, and had a hard, spare body, was the more forceful. Both were gentlemen on and off the pitch. They achieved a kind of mystical status.

My mother, God rest her, was convinced that if both were on the team, we couldn't be beaten. She wasn't far wrong.

I didn't come to know John Joe until after his playing days. Our first meeting was by chance, kind of . . .

I was cycling on my own to the Munster final in Killarney. John Joe was also on his own. I spotted him in front of me in the village of Farranfore. I put on a spurt and caught up with him at the bottom of Knockaderry Hill. We travelled the last eight miles together.

Even though Kerry lost to Cork that day, incidentally with Tim on the team, I remember the occasion fondly. Not only had I walked with greatness – I had cycled with greatness.

I came to know John Joe well in later years: I was in the pig business in a modest way, and he drove a lorry for the Co-op in Tralee – and was at the market in Castle Island every Monday morning.

On most Friday evenings he took his lorry with a load of bacon to the docks in Cork. It was often midnight when he got back as far as Castle Island. By then his journey was almost at an end.

Invariably, he called into McGillicuddy's in the Latin quarter, the most intimate bar in the known world. There he took his ease over a few bottles of stout.

There we had many a conversation: it wasn't all about Football – far from it.

John Joe was born in 1907 but I could never think of him as being old. I will remember him for his erect shoulders and his light step and the face that was always ready for a smile.

He had a happy family life and a fabulous Football career. To me he was a symbol of fulfilment in an age when Patrick Kavanagh's *The Great Hunger* was a metaphor that went for beyond the stony grey soil of Monaghan.

Magill, October 2001

ON THE ROAD

I was in good company in a café in Madrid with Eoin Hand, the Republic's manager, Billy Young of Bohemians and Charlie Stuart of the *Irish Press*.

We were watching Brazil and Italy on the television; we would see the winners in the flesh in the next round. We were confident that Brazil would come through; we looked forward to seeing them with their own eyes.

The score was level with ten minutes to go; Brazil half-cleared a corner kick. It mightn't have mattered if Junior, the most experienced player in the world, had moved out. His concentration lapsed; he stayed back and put Paolo Rossi onside.

And that stoat in human shape scored what proved to be the winning goal. Back in the café in Madrid we were very sad. We had been looking forward in anticipation, like small boys awaiting our first circus; now it wouldn't be coming at all.

Do you remember Ted Walsh on the occasion of Papillon's return from Aintree? 'As long as I live, I will never remember this day.' I felt the same about the semi-final between France and West Germany in those Spanish Finals in 1982.

The plane from Madrid flew low over fields of wheat and barley and giant sunflowers. It was my first time in the capital of Andalucia. I loved the cabs drawn by horses with bright flowers on their bridles – this for me made Seville unique.

And I remembered the immortal Philip Greene's immortal words as he ended his commentary after we had been devastated by Spain long ago: 'Seville where they get the oranges – but for us only the bitter lemon.'

There was a heatwave that Midsummer in the Western Mediterranean; the temperature that night was at an unreal figure which I forget. The fierce heat should have slowed down the game; it seemed to increase it. There was madness in the air that night.

You could say that the game was tempestuous and tumultuous, dramatic and melodramatic and tragic – and yet feel that your words were hopelessly inadequate.

Many will remember it most vividly for Harald Schumacher's 'tackle' on Patrick Batiston.

As the French right-back brought the ball into the penalty area, the keeper's short-arm 'challenge' kocked him unconscious. France lost a two-goal lead in extra time; to compound their misery, they were beaten in the penalty shoot-out. Incidentally, the keeper's foul was not punished.

Spanish airports are bad at the best of times; on that night in Seville the extra time and the shoot-out caused chaos. Somehow I got back to Madrid in time to get on the phone to the good old *Evening Press*.

I remember all too well how hopeless I felt as I tried to capture the essence of the most enthralling game of any kind that I had ever seen.

When it was all over that night in Seville, a visiting American who had seen his first game of Soccer looked at me in wonder. He said: 'Is it always like this?' How could I answer? I said: 'Sometimes it is.'

West Germany had only two days to recuperate from their ordeal; it was not surprising that they looked weary in the final. Italy could afford to miss a penalty and yet they won going away.

Who was the Man of the Match? Who was the Man of the Tournament? The gods who deal the cards had a quiet laugh.

In the run-up to the Finals, the stoat in human shape had been convicted of throwing games. His inclusion in the Italian squad caused a hurricane of indignation. The management persisted. And the man who went to Spain a villain came home a hero, kind of . . .

Mexico was a wonderful experience: we came to know a people as proud as they are poor – and as full of vitality as they are short of earthly goods. It was a miracle that the Finals went ahead there. In September of the previous year two violent earthquakes had rocked Mexico City.

The government played down the extent of the damage: they told the world that two thousand people had perished – the true figure was nearer twenty thousand. The government gambled on having every facility in time for the games: the Post Office engineers were still putting in the phones in the Azteca Stadium as the first match tipped off.

The football throughout the Finals was generally good. The meeting of Argentina and England is best-remembered – not for all the right reasons. Diego Maradona's goal which came after he had turned three defenders into pillars of stone is enmeshed in folklore.

His other goal is part of folklore too, if on a different shelf. Somehow the referee and the two linesmen believed that a man of five feet four could outjump a keeper of six feet one. In that crazy moment you could say that Maradona became the highest-paid handballer in history.

I doubt if Diego is Peter Shilton's favourite person.

That evening I travelled up to Los Angeles and then to Las Vegas, still disbelieving what I had seen in the Azteca Stadium. Some of my friends had told me that I would hate that city in the desert of Nevada. I loved the crazy place, though I doubt if I would care to live there.

The fight between Stevie Cruz and Barry McGuigan went on in the kind of heat we had experienced on that night in Seville. The bout was over in fifteen three-minute rounds; both men showed heroic endurance.

Barry was almost unconscious in the last round but Stevie was too chivalrous to knock him out. About midnight I sent back my report to the *Evening Press* and went to bed but couldn't sleep.

I went down to the bar about four. Jimmy Keaveney and Paddy Cullen had it all to themselves. We banished our woes. On the morrow, I was back in Mexico City for the final of the tournament, two days away.

On the eve of the event, it seemed for a few moments that there would be no final at all. I was in a bar in the middle of Mexico City when there was a violent upheaval. The whole world seemed to shake.

I was certain that it was El Temblor, 'The Earthquake'. I feared that Mexico City would disappear from the face of the earth and take me with it.

It was not El Temblor. It was an electrical storm, of the kind that we do not know on this island.

The final was good. West Germany made a brilliant late comeback from two goals down. Little Diego made the goal that won the Cup.

I have an especial memory of the journey back. It was about dawn as the plane began the descent to Gatwick. Below us we could see the coast of West Cork laid out like a great map.

My mind lingered over the inlets and headlands that I knew and loved so well.

Soon Tuskar Rock was on the port side and the plane was gliding towards Sussex, where I had worked when all the world was young. It was a real homecoming.

Our arrival in Cagliari Airport for Italy and the Islands and the Finals of 1990 was black comedy. Every policeman and soldier in Sardinia seemed to be on the tarmac. They were armed as if for battle.

Their presence was rather unnecessary but it put manners on our lads – there was no craic as we queued at the passport desk. Sardinia, however, wasn't all bad: the Republic won a splendid draw against England.

Then there was Genoa. We were billeted in Rapallo, on the Italian Riviera. It was beautiful. On the morning of our game with Romania I found myself in the television room of the Hotel Bristol with Jack Charlton and Paul McGrath.

We were watching the full video of Romania's most recent game. Jack surprised me by taking copious notes. When it was all over, he turned to us and said: 'Well . . . ' Paul said nothing. I said: 'Hagi'. Jack said: 'We'll close him down.'

After Packie had saved and David had scored, we were back in the Hotel Bristol. The night was surprisingly quiet – unlike the crazy aftermath of our victory over England in Stuttgart in the Euro Cup. When the lights went out in my bedroom, I had to phone back to Dublin from a cubby under the stairs. It was a labour of love.

The final in that tournament in Rome was a sad night for Argentina: they were woefully shorn by suspensions and injuries. Nevertheless, Germany had to labour to beat them; they won with a late, disputed penalty.

A few minutes after the final whistle, I was within touching distance of Diego Maradona as he was being interviewed. It was hard to believe that this little man with the unshaven, tear-stained face was one of the greatest players in the world.

The Finals in the US went ahead despite fierce opposition – and proved to be a resounding success. The organisation reminded us that the absence of fuss is the hallmark of intelligence.

The Republic began marvellously: the victory was over Italy in the Giants' Stadium was one of the most memorable in our football history. Alas, the game against Holland in Orlando was a sad anticlimax. We gave away two absurd goals. It was a bad way to go.

I am not complaining: I was privileged to be with the Republic at the Euro Finals and four World Cups.

Now my best wishes go with our marvellous back-up army as they travel from the Land of the Rising Prices to the Land of the Rising Sun.

Acknowledgements

The publishers would like to thank *Eircom Live* and *Magill* magazines and the *Sunday World*, where some of the pieces in this book first appeared.